Reincarnation For The Christian

QUEST BOOKS
are published by
The Theosophical Society in America,
a branch of a world organization
dedicated to the promotion of brotherhood and
the encouragement of the study of religion,
philosophy, and science, to the end that man may
better understand himself and his place in
the universe. The Society stands for complete
freedom of individual search and belief.
In the Theosophical Classics Series
well-known occult works are made
available in popular editions.

Cover art by *Jane A. Evans*

Reincarnation for the Christian

Quincy Howe Jr.

*This publication made possible with
the assistance of the Kern Foundation*

**The Theosophical Publishing House
Wheaton, Ill. U.S.A.
Madras, India/London, England**

The Theosophical Publishing House
306 West Geneva Road
Wheaton, IL 60187

A publication of the Theosophical Publishing House, a department of the Theosophical Society in America.

Library of Congress Cataloging in Publication Data

Howe, Quincy, 1934-
   Reincarnation for the Christian.

   Reprint. Originally published: Philadelphia, Westminster Press, 1974.
   Bibliography: p.
   1. Christianity and reincarnation.   I. Title.
BR115.R4H69   1987   236'.2   87-40132
ISBN 0-8356-0626-0 (pbk.)

Printed in the United States of America

For Edith,
whose idea it was

CONTENTS

PREFACE

This book was written out of the conviction that the world's great religions are now rushing toward a convergence of doctrine and practice such as would have been unthinkable at any other time in history. The life of the spirit, no less than that of the mind and body, is caught in a paroxysm of headlong change. Barriers of tradition, race, and language dissolve as the network of electronic media and jet travel draws men together. In science, politics, and the arts every innovation is weighed at once against an international array of competitors. No theory is so sacred, no method so established that it can exempt itself from outside influence.

Over the two thousand years of its existence Christianity has resolutely defined its mission and beliefs in terms of the Old and New Testaments and the authority of Christian tradition. Such a hermetic and insular approach does not accord well, however, with the ecumenical spirit of the present age. The time is ripe for Christians to ponder without reservation ideas that once seemed bizarre and alien. This does not mean that Christianity should abandon its past and rush heedlessly into change for change's sake. The result would be a formless amalgam of Eastern religions, popular philosophies, and scientific optimism. It does mean, however, that Christians should be as receptive in their spiritual life as they are in other areas to ideas that stand as undisputed truths in non-Christian parts of the world.

It should be apparent in the ensuing pages that I personally believe in the doctrine of reincarnation and feel that it can enhance the framework of Christian life. I am further convinced that the contemporary Christian is not so inflexible as to reject out of hand a belief that has been attested for nearly three thousand years. It is my purpose here to provide the historical and theological perspectives within which to view a doctrine that deserves serious consideration by all thoughtful Christians.

Q. H., JR.

Claremont, California

DOCTRINE
AND THE RELIGIOUS LIFE

My intention in this book is to propose to the serious Christian a belief that was indirectly anathematized by the church more than fourteen hundred years ago. Given the resistance within Christianity to heterodoxy of any sort, this may appear to be presumptuous. Indeed, distrust of heterodoxy is almost as old as Christianity, for since its beginnings the church has exercised a steady vigilance over doctrine. The major doctrinal assumptions of Christendom rest in turn upon the works of powerful and penetrating thinkers who devoted their lives to casting out beliefs that might diminish or distort the conclusions to be drawn from the life and ministry of Jesus Christ.

Since one of the traditional marks of the Christian has been his discernment in matters of doctrine, I shall start by saying a few words about the relationship between doctrine and the religious life. Specifically my question is: How far can one deviate from the accepted norms of Christian belief without threatening the very source and substance of his religious life? Upon reducing the Christian life to its bare essentials one discovers that doctrine itself is not the first concern of the Christian and that he can live a life in Christ and subject to the will of the Father within a very broad range of beliefs. If indeed this can be taken as the essence of Christianity— a life in Christ and subject to the will of the Father—then there are many things that take precedence over doctrine.

One may engage in worship, good works, prayer, love toward his neighbor—all without giving a thought to doctrine. The awareness of God as the ground of one's being and the cultivation of a life that will be pleasing in his sight are both preliminary to doctrine. Indeed, doctrine arises out of the attempt to analyze the religious life and derive conclusions and instructions from what first must exist as a state of awareness and unnamed force in the individual life.

This is not to say that doctrine is something which the Christian may disregard entirely. It may be defined as what the church teaches and the individual confesses, and its importance lies in establishing those articles of faith to which one gives assent. For example, anyone calling himself a Christian is expected to subscribe to a belief in the forgiveness of sins. One of the functions that the church has taken upon itself is to draw these various articles of faith together into a well-ordered and logically consistent creed. The result of this activity is a system which the church proposes as normative. What the church has further maintained is that the individual's relationship with God is defective to the extent that he cannot assent to these normative creeds.

This is the point at which doctrine can become a pernicious force and undermine the very spirit that it proposes to nourish. Any attempt to measure a Christian by his orthodoxy—that is, by the extent to which he can accept the doctrine of the church—gives prominence to the products of the religious life rather than to its source. For example, the church and the Scriptures teach: "Thou shalt love the Lord thy God with thy whole heart, and with thy whole soul, and with thy whole strength, and with thy whole mind; and thy neighbor as thyself." (Luke 10:27.) Until one has felt the love of God rising in his own heart, however, this remains no more than a hollow and lifeless injunction. So too with the love for one's neighbor: it is plausible only as an experience. All such Scriptural commands and creedal assumptions arise and become meaningful as the by-product of something else, and it is finally this something else which imparts to the religious life meaning and power.

Unfortunately many Christians find that doctrine plays an ambiguous and occasionally even obstructive role in their religious life. Very often the religious life begins for them with statements of creed and doctrine rather than the experience of which doctrine is the remote reflection. Their religious life can be likened to a complex pattern of lines intersecting at such disparate points as "died on the cross," "atoned for our sins," "triune God," "the resurrection of the body." The tension between these points has always been both the fascination and the despair of the Christian—an exquisite sense of paradox that challenges faith and humbles the intellect.

This has been very beneficial to the extent that it has provided Christianity with a massive literature and vocabulary to account for God's ways with man. It has been detrimental, however, to the extent that for many it has deflected their attention from the religious life to purely speculative and philosophical matters. Thus many a Christian, when confronted with novel and unorthodox ideas such as reincarnation, will automatically refer them to his theological system rather than to his personal sentiments. If they do not conform with his theology, he will probably dismiss them without further consideration. Unable or unwilling to refer to their own intuitions, such Christians have thoughtlessly rejected much in the name of orthodoxy.

The Christian, however, who has had intuitions or experiences that seem to support the heterodox finds his situation uncomfortable and frustrating, for the doctrine of the church tells him he is wrong, while his own inner voice assures him of the contrary. The solution that I propose to this quandary is to relax the rule of orthodoxy long enough to examine reincarnation on its own merits. In saying this I do not mean that I can "prove" reincarnation, as one proves that the world is round, nor do I propose to sweep out every notion of doctrine. I merely propose that the Christian momentarily suspend the dictates of orthodoxy and consider the premise of reincarnation. If he remains unconvinced at the end, he has lost nothing and probably has gained some insight into the doctrinal posture of traditional Christianity. If he should be persuaded that reincarnation can be brought into harmony with Christianity, he will have clarification and guidance for many matters that have been either avoided or relegated to the area of "mystery" by conventional orthodoxy.

At this point the reader may object that my approach defies Christianity's historical self-consciousness. The church has always inclined toward the view that there is an ongoing process of doctrinal revelation taking place. Thus the history of Christianity is studded with moments when God made disclosures about himself and his workings. Accordingly, the posture and doctrine of the church at present are determined by the accumulation of these revelatory moments, and the sequence of these moments constitutes a sacred history. Christianity possesses to a unique degree this veneration for its past. The entire evolution and articulation of doctrine is seen as the result of a continuously productive dispensation. Seen in this light, my suggestion to suspend orthodoxy for the moment could perhaps be condemned as irreverent.

What right can anyone claim to ask the followers of a religion with a sacred history to suspend all thought of tradition? My answer is that in place of the conservatism that arises out of a sacred tradition, the church now needs, more than ever, the flexibility that goes with an open mind. The confrontation between past and present has been amply illustrated by the difficulty that Catholics have been having over the issue of birth control. The views of Augustine on the ends of marriage are not necessarily adequate to the mid-twentieth century. Recent developments suggest that the church of the future is not going to be the church militant of the past. The specific issue of reincarnation is quite immaterial here; it is a matter of creating an attitude that does not stand in abject servitude to the past. The Christianity of the future will stand or fall on its ability to evoke that experiential impetus which precedes theology. Once the Christian can fix his eye on this impetus, the originator of the religious life, then doctrinal matters will fall into place with a spontaneous and natural ease.

Now as never before the Christian church is being called upon to prove its flexibility and responsiveness to change. An institution whose traditions are sacred and whose doctrines are revealed truth is being besieged from all sides by new philosophies, both sacred and profane. Some of these are openly antagonistic to organized religion, whereas others have an ambivalent impact. While I certainly do not suggest that the survival of the church depends upon its willingness to accept reincarnation, I do believe that the issue provides a case study of the kind of modern heresy that the church is going to be forced to confront. Some of these modern heresies may have the potential to give the church a much-needed infusion of vitality. Perhaps this will prove to be true of reincarnation. Others, such as the utopian promises of the drug culture, could very easily unravel entirely the religious fabric of our civilization.

In the pages that follow I use Augustine as the chief spokesman of orthodoxy against whom I argue the case for reincarnation, and it may seem that I am needlessly hard on him. There is nothing either gratuitous or vindictive in my choice of Augustine, however. I have used him in this way because, of the fathers of the church, he more than any other at once understood Platonism and yet perceived the line that divides it from orthodoxy. This is most significant, for the case for reincarnation, at least in the West, has come to us through Plato's views on the soul and the afterlife, and the extent to which reincarnation was known in the Greco-Roman world was due largely to Plato. At those moments when Christianity moved close to a reincarnationist view—most notably among the fathers from Alexandria—it was under the influence of Platonism.

Augustine, like many of the fathers of the church, first accepted and understood Christianity largely in terms of Platonism. Unlike some of his predecessors, however, he was able to pare away those layers of Platonism which might obscure or distort orthodoxy. As a result of the great acumen and penetration he applied to this task, he arrived in his later years at a statement of Christianity that displayed with unique clarity the heterodoxy of Platonism.

As I try in these pages to review the case for reincarnation, I find myself confronted again and again by the brilliance and authority of Augustine. I quote him with a full appreciation of this and with the hope that he would find my effort, not impudent, but salutary to the untiring effort of Christianity to define and redefine its basic assumptions.

In the twentieth century the great non-Christian world religions such as Hinduism, Buddhism, and Mohammedanism demand our respect and recognition. The ecumenical spirit of the present is forcing Christians to take cognizance of other world saviors and other doctrines. Ultimately this must lead to change within Christianity. Orthodoxy had its day when the very survival of the church depended upon combating Donatism, Marcionism, Pelagianism, Arianism, and the many other heresies of early Christianity. Indeed, the church survived because of this very ability to identify what was extraneous and suppress it. This rigorous sense of orthodoxy that once vindicated Christian truth in the midst of conflicting and rival orthodoxies has now performed its task. What the church needs at the present is not defenders of the faith but revivers of the faith—not necessarily the faith of the Nicene Creed, but a faith that will impart vitality and significance to the religious life.

The measure of such a faith is not going to be its orthodoxy, but its capacity to arouse Christians to a life in Christ. If the price that must be paid for such a faith is to compromise the orthodoxy of traditional Christianity, I believe that the gain will have been infinitely greater than the loss.

What is at stake at every moment in the life of a religion is the extent to which the individual follower finds the presence of God manifest in his own life. Once this is lost, whatever orthodoxy remains is no more than the fossilized trace of something now defunct.

I would hope that the forward-looking and open-minded Christian will bear these thoughts in mind as he ponders the implications of reincarnation. The only indulgence I ask of my reader is that he be "irreverent" long enough to consider the appeal of reincarnation, some reasons why people have believed in it, and its possible place within Christianity.

I

REINCARNATION: THE BASIC THEORY

There have been many Western apologists for the doctrine of reincarnation, and their works are widely available. As far as I know, however, there has been no attempt to provide a full and systematic account based upon the classic exponents of reincarnation—the ancient Indians and the Platonists.

There is a voluminous esoteric literature on reincarnation and this has its place and legitimacy. Men and women such as Edgar Cayce, Arthur Ford, Gina Cerminara, and Jeane Dixon have done much to contribute toward knowledge and acceptance of reincarnation. I shall not be making reference to them in this book, however, since it is my purpose to render as explicitly as possible the theological and metaphysical assumptions upon which the doctrine of reincarnation is based. The strange stories of past lives and the lavish vistas of the abode between lives make fascinating reading, but such things belong to the spiritualistic side of reincarnation, not to the theory itself.

The doctrine of reincarnation provides the script for a drama of cosmic proportions: it accounts for the source of the individual soul, the demands and conditions for its self-improvement, and the final goal of its journey. Some of the most profound and powerful thinkers in the history of man have embraced reincarnation, and the result of their labors is an extraordinarily comprehensive and explicit account of human destiny in relation to the Absolute. Entire dimensions of the soul's progress that have remained shrouded in mystery within traditional orthodoxy are laid open and accounted for by the theory of reincarnation.

Origin of the Soul

The entire cycle of individuated life commences at the point when God differentiates and diversifies his Being. Whereas orthodoxy speaks of God as creating the world *ex nihilo,* out of nothing, those who have accepted reincarnation are inclined to speak of an act of emanation rather than an act of creation. Our traditional Christian view of creation envisions God fashioning the cosmos out of the void, something alien to himself. There is already a rather troublesome contradiction here, in that the void (which is by definition empty) is providing the stuff of creation. For both the Hindu and the Neoplatonist the formula is somewhat different. God has two modes of being: quiescent and manifesting. When he goes from quiescence to manifestation, he simply extends and diversifies his being into the myriad forms of physical and ideational creation. One such form that emanates from God is the human soul. This theory of emanation entails neither paradox nor contradiction, for if God is omnipresent and all-pervasive, there cannot be anything that does not partake of his Being. Thus the reincarnationist would describe the cosmos, not as a creation, but as an emanation from God. Plotinus, the third-century Neoplatonist, is one of the most penetrating exponents of emanation. In his view the entire cosmos is the extension of God, or the One, as he calls it. Here is a typical passage describing the process of diversification that gives rise to the physical world.

> In this dance of life the soul looks upon the font of life, the font of intelligence, the origin of existence, the foundation of goodness, and the roots of its own being. These phenomena do not physically flow out from the One, nor do they diminish the One,

for the One does not consist of substance. If it weie substance, then its emanations would be subject to corruption. However, they are eternal. This is because the One itself always remains the same, nor does it become fragmented into its emanations. It remains ever entire. Thus the emanations always remain, just as light abides as long as the sun itself persists. (*Enneads* 6.9.9.)

Plotinus is never easy to follow, and this passage is no exception. Working back from the conclusion of the passage, one finds that the simile about the sun and its light is helpful. If you can envision a beam of light that has consciousness of itself and latent consciousness of its source, you have a fair analogy for Plotinus' view of the soul and the One. By the mere act of shining, a source of light neither loses anything from its own substance nor does it create something which is alien or different from itself. In its complete and utter self-sufficiency, it simply shines, and the light that it radiates is its extension. Thus, just as the beams are in their essence light, so the soul in its essence is divine.

The dynamics of the world's coming into being as described by Plotinus shares some features with the Christian concept and yet also shows some important differences. For both, God is the cause and origin of all. The theory of Plotinus, however, does not present us with the paradox of God spinning whole galaxies out of nothing. For Plotinus the entire cosmos is no more than the inevitable and natural overflow of God. Just as light and heat are the inevitable overflow of fire, so too souls, life, and intelligence are the necessary overflow of God's being.

This distinction between the view of Plotinus and that of orthodoxy at once introduces a major difference between the reincarnationist and traditional Christian views of man. For the Christian, since man is created out of nothing, he does not actually participate directly in God's being and nature; he may only achieve vicarious participation through the Son, God's intermediary. Man as the creature of the void, or a ball of clay in Genesis, can never achieve more than an adoptive relationship with God, even though he be made in God's image. Man's fall, damnation, and final separation from God are all possible in a view that allows him no more than an adoptive relationship. With the account of Plotinus, however, that which emanates from the sun also partakes fully of the sun's essence, which is light. Following the simile of Plotinus, one can say that the light of the individual soul is of a lesser intensity than the light of God. Qualitatively, however, the light is the same, whether it is viewed at its source or at some great remove. By this analogy the individual soul contains the attributes of God. Thus perfect love, wisdom, and joy are just as innate to the soul as heat and light are to the sun. Man in his essence possesses the latent capacity to express the fullness of God's attributes.

This concept of Plotinus is similar to the ancient Indian theory of Brahman and Atman. According to Vedanta, the consummation of Vedic doctrine, every human being consists in essence of a divine Self, the Atman, which is the indwelling God. The goal of the spiritual life is to realize the full and perfect identity between this Atman and Brahman, who is God as the unmanifest Absolute.

The Fall of the Soul

The question that immediately arises out of this theory of divine emanation is: How can the Atman, or divine essence, lapse into incarnate existence and forget its divine nature? This in fact is one of the paradoxes with which theologians have always struggled. Why would God allow anything that comes from himself to live in partial estrangement from himself? If perfect love is to be counted as one of God's attributes, then one may indeed be puzzled at the sight of hapless and benighted man experiencing heartbreak again and again in his attempts to penetrate the mystery of life. The answer to this problem for the conventional Christian is that in the Garden of Eden man wantonly chose to defy

God. The result was a fall from grace into a state of alienation from God. Then the drama of salvation and the incarnation of Christ are arranged by God to bring about man's reconciliation with himself. It is because of man's fallen state and the willfulness inherited by all the sons of Adam that the choice for God is so difficult and true happiness so elusive.

The story of Adam and Eve provides a satisfying and profound account of man's lapsed condition. It allows both for free will—man's choice to eat the fruit—and the power of God's grace—all those reminders he sends to make the choice for himself more real and attractive.

The proponents of reincarnation have no less subtle ways of dealing with the same problem. In order to be fully satisfying, any account of the fall is going to have to make room for the exercise of free will and the pull of God's grace. Whereas the traditional Christian falls from a state of innocent conciliation with God into one of partial estrangement, the reincarnationist has fallen from a state of God-consciousness to one of partial forgetfulness. Considering that the Self for the reincarnationist is seen as pure divinity, the only lapse can be one of defective self-awareness. To use the vocabulary of Christianity, when fully in the "Eden-state," the Atman or soul is able to cognize itself as Brahman or God. At some point, however, the Self loses the ability to cognize itself as divine, and this is the point at which the fall for the reincarnationist takes place.

Plato, who wrote in the fourth century B.C., developed a very full and explicit doctrine of reincarnation. In his dialogue *Phaedrus* (247–248) he recounts a very enlightening myth to account for the self-willed fall of the soul. He envisions the disincarnate soul as tripartite and likens it to a charioteer (man's reason), a noble, white, winged horse (man's spirited and energetic tendencies), and an unruly, black, winged horse (man's concupiscent and passionate tendencies). As long as the charioteer has control of the horses, the soul flies through the heavens with the gods and contemplates their attributes

of justice, temperance, beauty, and knowledge. It happens to
some, however, that the intemperate horse gets out of hand
and the soul veers down from its divine circuit. If it declines
far enough, the soul will finally lose its wings entirely and
plunge into the much grosser and more debased state of incarnate existence.

This metaphor has certain similarities with that of Eden.
The discriminative power of the charioteer loses control and
gives in to the intemperate horse. Likewise, the discriminative
powers of Adam and Eve give way before temptation. In
both cases divine conciliation or contemplation was forfeited
when the will was no longer strong enough to enforce reason
and temperance. The quality of the Platonic fall is such that
the soul can no longer enjoy the vision of divinity and must
travail to regain its wings.

Again India offers a somewhat similar account of man's
separation from God. Instead of willing his fall, however, man
became so enmeshed in the tumultuous activity of creation
that he lost sight of his divine nature. That which obscures
man's view of his own divinity is called *māyā*, a Sanskrit word
indicating the divine spell that God casts on creation to give
it the appearance of separate and distinct reality. Lord
Krishna, speaking of this power of *māyā* in the *Bhagavad-
Gita*, describes it as follows:

It is indeed hard to go beyond this divine spell (*māyā*) of
mine, as it pervades the very fundament of creation. But who-
ever takes refuge in me penetrates this divine spell. (*Bhagavad-
Gita* 14.7.)

What these lines proclaim is that God casts, not an impenetrable spell on creation, but an opaque one. This means
that the man who makes the proper effort will surely succeed
in recognizing his separation from God as an illusion and the
impression of fragmentation and estrangement as a deception. All is one, just as heat and light are both one with the
sun.

Any system that insists upon the divinity of man raises the vexing question: Given man's inherent divinity, what is to prevent him from realizing it at once? The answer for Plato is the intemperate horse of passion that constantly draws the soul down from its divine abode. The ancient Indians, on the other hand, see the soul as momentarily beguiled by the specious reality of the created world. These accounts are not mutually exclusive and are similar to the extent that they depict the divine Self as temporarily confused about its true nature.

Samskāras: Traces from the Past

If the Self is an eternal spark of God, one might well ask how much continuity there can be from one life to another. Is it only the pure divine spark that proceeds through the cycles of rebirth, or does a larger residue from life's experiences make the journey as well? Does the entire personality with all its strengths and weaknesses manifest again and again in different bodies, or does that particle of divinity pass on, abandoning the personality as so much excess baggage?

If reincarnation is to have ethical force, the soul must retain some residue from one life to another. Otherwise each life will have to be a fresh start without any accumulation from the past. Indeed, one of the most powerful arguments that the reincarnationists advance in favor of their belief is that the Self is going through a cumulative education. Although the recollection of past lives is apparently lost, one is forever followed by the fruits of his works. Although Platonism is vague on this matter, the sacred literature of India is very specific. Our works—whatever we have done throughout the ages of time—are eternally engraved into the soul. If, in fact, one were to define the personality as the accumulation of everything one has done, then it can indeed be said that the personality survives from one life to another. Here is a statement from the *Upanishads* on this:

As the body is augmented by food and water, so the individual
self, augmented by its aspirations, sense contact, visual impressions, and delusion, assumes successive forms in accordance
with its actions. (*Svetasvatara Upanishad* 5.11.)

Typical of Indian scripture, this sentence is so terse that
pages of commentary could be written on it. The analogy to
the body and food is very illuminating and provides the basis
for an entire theory of personality. At any given point of its
existence the physical body is no more than the product of
the nourishment it has received. In like manner, the individual personality can be viewed as no more than the sum
of all its previous experiences, ambitions, and entanglements
with delusion. This means that not only the divine spark
proceeds from one body to another but in fact the recollection and resultant wisdom of all that it has undergone makes
the journey. This is recollection, not in the sense of impressions
directly available to the memory, but rather in the sense of
retaining the special poignancy of each individual experience.
For example, if a person has experienced profound grief and
tragedy in a certain incarnation, he will carry with him whatever sensitivity and wisdom this grief may have brought into
being.

Nothing is lost in the many cycles of reincarnation, neither
the self-assurance born of success nor the patient strength
born of sorrow. Although our power of recall cannot conjure
up the specific events, their fruits, which are no less than the
total personality, are never lost.

There is even a word in Sanskrit to describe the traits that
move on from one life to another. It is *samskāra*, and its basic
meaning is the mental impressions left by causes no longer
operative. Indeed, according to the *Yoga Sutras* of Patanjali
(3.18), the advanced spiritual aspirant can recover at will
the experiences that gave rise to these mental impressions.
Regardless of whether these experiences are available to our
consciousness, however, or lie buried in the hidden recesses

of memory, the *samskāras* follow us from one life to another.

This means that such qualities as driving ambition, a hot temper, special aptitudes, generosity, or miserliness all follow one from life to life. Seen in this light, the character is far from being the mere accumulation of the environmental influences of one life. There exist much more basic propensities upon which environment will have only a partial effect. For example, the tendency to compassion can be nourished by kind and thoughtful parents, but if the tendency is strong enough from previous lives, it will come out even with mean and niggardly parents. This also means that the extraordinary aptitude of child prodigies is simply the result of skills acquired in earlier lives. For the reincarnationist, there is the comfort of knowing that every improvement of character or ability achieved in this life will follow him through the ages.

The economy of the cosmos is very tidy, and the fruits of any effort, no matter how great or small, never leave the soul. In all that we achieve we are acquiring a treasure that will continue to serve us through the recurring cycles of lives. One's character is a great repository of virtues and faults, and neither can weakness that has been overcome trouble us in future lives, nor will newly won strength desert us.

The Ascent of the Soul

Since the soul carries with it the accumulation of all previous lives, it naturally follows that each individual is going to either advance or regress. This personality which clings to us always is either going to grow more compassionate, sensitive, and intelligent through good works and noble aspirations or else it is going to become more brutish through selfish and thoughtless acts. Herein lies one of the great attractions of reincarnation: it allows for and indeed demands personal evolution. If the soul is constantly undergoing new experiences, then the totality of one's personality will be subject to constant change. The individual is traversing an evolutionary course that spans many lives; according to his actions he is either retreating from his true nature as spirit or advancing toward the divine goal.

If the cycle of creation arises when God extends himself into manifestation, then the natural goal and end of this cycle is going to be the moment when God absorbs everything back into himself. For the reincarnationist the fall of man amounts to no more than forgetfulness of his divine origin and identity. As far as the evolution of the personality is concerned, one is making progress as long as he is acquiring characteristics that manifest his nature as divinity. He will be backsliding, however, to the extent that he suppresses his divine nature and affirms in thought and action his separation from God. Such is the belief of reincarnationists both in the East and in the West.

Thus for Plato, just as the fall of the soul is a loss of wings, so the ascent of the soul entails the restoration of these wings. The progress of every man depends upon his ability to ascend from the intemperate and base pleasures deriving from the physical realm to those pure pleasures of spirit and universal beauty which feed the soul. (*Phaedrus* 251A–B.) To the extent that he succeeds in this, the soul recovers its wings and becomes able to rise to the realms where the gods hold their procession. The pattern of growth for all is to wean themselves away from these inferior distractions and fix their attention upon that which calls to mind the supernal ideal of beauty—a task that requires many incarnations.

In the sacred literature of India the thralldom of the soul is defined in somewhat different terms. Unenlightened man, as he passes through the experience of incarnations, labors under a false sense of identity. Instead of seeing himself as the divine Atman, or Self, he attributes ultimate significance to the ambitions, sensations, and desires that arise out of his physical experiences. Thus, rather than seeing himself as an emanation of the Absolute, he sees himself as the product of education, family, and culture; the totality of his life becomes the achievement of goals, the enjoyment of pleasure, and the avoidance of pain within these limits. Sanskrit employs the term *kāmas* to describe the attachment or desire that compels one to pursue all of these goals. The divine Self is obscured by the smaller self of worldly achievement and pleasure, and this smaller self in turn is propelled from one pursuit to another by *kāmas*, or attachment.

The soul is drawn back to incarnations, not by divine injunction, but simply by the urge to fulfill desires arising out of worldly life. For example, a man may have a burning desire to gain worldly fame through the works of his intellect. Again and again this desire will bring him back to a body, for this ambition clearly cannot be attained by the disincarnate self with neither a body to express itself nor other men to acclaim it. In order for the Self to cut its ties with physical incarnation, *kāmas* must be removed. This can be done either along the slow and arduous path of feeding desires until disgust and satiety set in or by the much quicker and more efficient route of recognizing the ultimate vanity of such desires. This concept is very well illustrated by the following passage from the *Bhagavad-Gita*:

> [Arjuna asks:]
> What is it now that constrains man to commit sin, O Krishna, as though compelled by force and against his will?
> The Blessed Lord answered:
> It is this desire, this anger that is born of the passionate constituents of creation. Know that here in this world desire is your foe, all-consuming, all-sinful. As a fire is obscured by smoke, as a mirror by dust, and as an embryo by the womb, so is all this [wisdom] obscured by passion. Wisdom, O Arjuna, is covered over by the manifestation of desire, the eternal enemy of the wise, and a fire that is never quenched. (*Bhagavad-Gita* 3.36–39.)

Not only does desire tie the individual to the pursuit of worldly goals, but it also shrouds and obscures his view of reality. Furthermore, anyone who devotes himself to appeasing his desires is merely throwing fuel upon a fire that can never be appeased.

Although this metaphor in the *Gita* is very different from the one used by Plato, there is a basic convergence of meaning. What happens to the incarnate soul of unenlightened man is that its occupations and ambitions sink below the horizon of its divine nature. As the Platonic soul forgets its divine abode and pursues inferior objectives, it becomes enmeshed in the quest of crude and ignoble gratification. To advance again, it must cultivate experiences and relationships that call to mind the ideal of beauty. There is no less of a thralldom than that described by Krishna in the *Gita*. In both cases the individual is under the false impression that the pursuit of physical or selfish pleasure will satisfy the deepest needs of his nature. It is a matter of moving from the demands of one's worldly and physical nature to those of the divine Self. For Plato, this means cultivating those things which remind us of divine beauty; in the *Gita*, it is a matter of leaving behind those passions and attractions which thwart and disturb the divine equanimity of the Self.

The Law of *Karma*

As the Self gradually comes free of its thralldom, it ascends, and then it can better its condition according to what the ancient Indians have called the Law of *Karma*. In its most literal sense, *karma* is an action noun meaning work or action. Specifically, it is the effect that takes place as the result of some prior activity. It comes from the Sanskrit root *"kṛ"* ("to do, to make") and is an abstract noun meaning "action" or "doing." Indeed, this etymology is very instructive, for one can say that *karma* is no more than that which a man has done. In a more general sense, *karma* is the inevitable succession of cause and effect that governs existence at all levels. The principle expounded in Newton's Third Law of Motion (i.e., for every action there is an equal and opposite reaction) obtains not just in the sphere of mechanics and physics but in the life of the emotions, the mind, and the spirit. Every thought or deed acts upon the equilibrium of the universe and calls for a response in kind. It is not just insensate matter that is buffeted back and forth between cause and effect; the very harmony of all creation is under the same compulsion.

For the reincarnationist, *karma* is a matter of the utmost importance, for its authority extends through the many cycles of past lives. The reward for the good we do in the present may not come back until many lives hence, and the suffering that we endure here and now may very well be the outcome of some pernicious act done lifetimes ago. The retribution of *karma* is certain, but not necessarily immediate. The economy of spirit is no less tidy than that of physics and mechanics; it claims only the additional prerogative of coming to fulfillment, not instantly, but with the fullness of time.

The skeptic may ask how a balance sheet of our merits over many lives can be maintained. The reincarnationist need only answer: How else would you account for life's apparent injustice? Again and again we see the man who has spent an entire life in the pursuit of pleasure and who has trodden underfoot the happiness of his fellowman. As he reaches an advanced age, he expires amidst happiness and prosperity. Another person is born into the world with a debilitating and unsightly birth defect; for a few years he makes a piteous effort to survive, only to go off to an early grave, unloved and unnoticed by all. We reason that the selfish man will perhaps reap his punishment in some kind of afterlife, but our sense of justice is outraged at the sight of someone who never had a chance and collapses wretchedly in an effort that was doomed to failure.

Here is where the Law of *Karma* makes sense of the apparent nonsense of life. The man who is born into abject poverty may have made ill use of his wealth in an earlier life; the wealthy man is reaping the fruits of earlier generosity.

He who must express his humanity through a deformed and defective body may have maimed and disfigured others in lives now past. If a man has all the gifts of wealth, charm, and intelligence and then employs them for his own gain and to the hurt of others, he risks forfeiting these boons in a future life. In such a scheme there is no extreme of human life that does not have its natural cause.

Karma introduces an element of reason and logic into a problem that has vexed many a devout Christian. How are we to believe in a perfect and loving God if he persistently seems to place man in tragic and painful situations? What can the Christian pastor say to the mother of a defective child? Only that the counsels of God are hidden from man, so that he may learn to grow in faith. What of the millions of all ages who are daily dying of starvation? Lacking a direct and reasonable explanation for this, even the most faithful Christian is occasionally tempted to hold God responsible. It is indeed an exacting and hard test of faith for man to affirm the goodness of God while surrounded by misery and suffering.

The reincarnationist—who would surely respect such a faith—has quite a different solution. The Law of *Karma* entirely absolves God from responsibility for human suffering. Man assumes eternal and total responsibility for his life and has only his own egotism and bad judgment to thank for wretched and apparently unjust circumstances. God's love and justice are in no way impugned, for it is God who both ordains the Law of *Karma* and helps man to emerge triumphant at last from his hardships. As Plato says at the end of his *Republic*: "God is blameless; man has chosen his own fate" (617E).

As for the long lapse of time that may pass between cause and effect in the Law of *Karma*, the fruit of the act does not come until the individual is fully ready to receive it. Imagine that a brutal and savage man commits a murder. He may have much to learn in the way of compassion and righteousness before he can appreciate the monstrosity of his acts. Thus many lifetimes later, once he has grown in sympathy and sensitivity, he may inadvertently kill a man in an accident; only now that he has acquired moral sensibilities is he able to feel contrition appropriate to the original offense. The Law of *Karma* has been delayed until the personality has ripened sufficiently to assimilate a lesson which, until then, would have been too subtle for it to grasp. What remains constant throughout is the balance of justice.

Many Westerners regard Indian thought as encouraging a quietistic and otherworldly way of life. The implications of *karma*, however, show that this is not the case. The progress of each soul is involved in a mesh of action and reaction. The Law of *Karma* calls man to a life of dynamic activity— it is by action that we can redress the wrongs of the past and make our peace with God. Even though the soul may be in a deluded or fallen state of consciousness when confined to the world and the physical body, there is still laid upon every man the sacred obligation to work in the world.

There is an evolutionary tide along which the soul travels back toward God, and action is the sacred and visible evidence of man's exertions. Indeed, creation itself abhors inertia and urges man on to those acts which will hasten the spiritualization of his own life and of his immediate environment. Here is the *Gita* on the necessity of work:

> Not even for a moment can anyone remain free of action. Whether he wills it or not, every man is created to action by the very structure of the world. (*Bhagavad-Gita* 3.5.)

Every situation in which a man finds himself can finally be traced back to his *karma*. An apt illustration of this crops up in a most unexpected context when the church father Origen speaks of the "*karma*" of Jacob and Esau.

> Is there injustice with God? By no means! (Rom. 9:14.) A close look at the Scriptural account of Jacob and Esau will

show that there is no injustice with God. Although it is said
that before they were born or had done anything in this life,
the elder should serve the younger, still one finds no injustice
with God. Nor does one find injustice because Jacob sup-
planted his brother in the womb. We should only realize that
Jacob is so worthily loved by God on the merits of previous
lives and hence deserved precedence over his brother. (*On
First Principles* 2.9.7.)

Although it is perhaps unexpected to see *karma* in the
Christianity of third-century Alexandria where Origen was
educated, this passage is an excellent illustration. Jacob's
merits from past lives surpassed those of Esau and he was
rewarded accordingly.

The Question of Animal Incarnations

A widely debated question in the literature on reincarnation is whether man's soul passes through animal forms, and
critics of reincarnation have taken great offense at this. In
fact, the very first reference to reincarnation in the West is
a satiric poem by Xenophanes (born ca. 565 B.C.) concerning
the philosopher Pythagoras, who was a great advocate of
reincarnation.

They say that while walking past a dog that was being beaten,
Pythagoras took pity and said: "Stop, strike no more; it is the
soul of my friend—I recognize his voice." (Diogenes Laërtius,
Lives 8.8.20.)

For anyone who believes in the dignity of man, not to
mention his divinity, the notion of animal incarnations is
offensive. Moreover, the implications immediately strike one
as farcical and suggest laughable and absurd possibilities,
such as the one proposed above by Xenophanes.

Although there are overt and explicit references to animal
incarnations in Plato (e.g., *Phaedo* 82A–B, and *Phaedrus*

249B), he appears to abandon this belief in his later works. Indeed Proclus, one of Plato's major interpreters in antiquity, takes the animal incarnations entirely allegorically. Thus when Plato says that carnal and intemperate men are reborn as donkeys, while those who are temperate and industrious but lack philosophy will come back as bees or ants, he merely means that they will acquire an antlike or a donkeylike personality.

Likewise in India the Laws of Manu (12.9) as well as numerous passages in the *Upanishads* suggest the possibility of animal incarnations.

Transmigration, or the belief in animal incarnations, poses a serious theological problem. One of the basic premises of the reincarnationist is that man is a spark of divinity and that the entire purpose of human life is to give full manifestation to this spark. If this is the case, one cannot but feel that the capacity of an animal for expressing divinity is very severely limited. Such qualities as sympathy, moral discernment, and selflessness can only find full and adequate expression in a human being. Animal incarnations would seem to stultify the very purpose of man's spiritual evolution, as it would trap the divine spark in hopelessly confining forms of life. Given these considerations, the allegorical theory of Proclus mentioned above is especially attractive—that the animal incarnations should be taken as warnings to man not to sink into bestial conduct. Only in an extreme case might a man so abuse and deface his own humanity as to lose all claim to human incarnation.

The Interval Between Lives

Another question that naturally arises concerns the length of the disincarnate periods. There is such a disparity of opinions on this that it is almost impossible to come up with any consistent and well-founded answer. Although Plato proposes thousand-year cycles from birth to birth, this seems to be an arbitrary figure suggested in the interest of neatness and symmetry. More attractive is the suggestion that the length of repose between lives is in direct proportion to the virtue and spirituality of one's incarnate life (*Bhagavad-Gita* 6.41). Thus the intervals are seen as quiescent periods during which the soul recovers from its sorrows and mistakes and reaps the benefit of its good acts. There is a massive accumulation of literature on this from esoteric and spiritualist writers, and although the specific figures they propose are disparate and contradictory, they tend to support the doctrine of the *Gita* that souls are given rest in accordance with the virtue of their incarnate life.

Lapse of Memory

Critics of reincarnation argue that there surely should be some vestige of recollection from one life to another. However, with the exception of a very few extraordinary instances (see Chapter II), this does not prove to be the case. We must content ourselves with the answer that Plato proposes in the myth of Er at the end of the *Republic* (621C). Just before a soul is about to enter its new body, says Plato, it drinks the waters of forgetfulness and loses the recollection of all that had come before.

Disappointing as this may be to people who fancy that they have marched with Alexander the Great or been fed to the lions in ancient Rome, there are some practical considerations to make us thankful for oblivion of the past. For the average man the burden of mischief, guilt, and self-reproach acquired in one life is all that he can bear. Imagine if every offense, insult, and disgrace of many lives were weighing us down! Faced with such a prospect, anyone would agree it is a kind providence that enjoins the waters of forgetfulness.

Just because the memory of specific events is blotted out, this does not mean that the deeper wisdom gained from our past experiences is lost. The *samskāras*, those traces from former states of being, follow us from one life to another. Although our experiences themselves are lost in the transition, their significance is never lost.

Union: The End of the Cycle

The final stage in the progress of the soul is the full realization of the divinity from which it originally came. After the cycles of many lives—the exact number is indeterminate—man begins to manifest and become conscious of his divine nature. Purified first by the hard school of life and then by selfless works, worship, and the cultivation of God within, the individual self begins to penetrate the veil of *māyā*, to grow the wings that will lift the soul out of the disappointments and distractions of the phenomenal world. Man becomes increasingly fixed in the life of spirit and finds his attention turning more and more toward the divine. The things of the world have consequence only as they point to God. The man who is close to the end will begin to develop the gifts and qualities of saints and sages. Then at the very end of the cycles the individual will finally experience the fullness of divine union.

The state that heralds the emancipation of the individual soul from the compulsion of *karma* and necessity to incarnate has been variously described: union, bliss, *samādhi*, and ecstasy are some of the words associated with it. One could quote passages at great length and their variety would only show how inexhaustible divine bliss is. Here, just by way of illustration, is an especially vivid description from the Neoplatonist philosopher Plotinus.

Many times I have plunged into myself leaving the body behind, having passed beyond all else, and deep within myself. Then I see such an extraordinary beauty and am convinced that I belong to a mighty order of things. I live life at its peak and become one with the divine. Once firmly fixed in this state,

I come into that sphere of activity above all that is intelligible
and am transfixed within myself. (*Enneads* 4.8.1.)

At the end of the soul's journey the individual discovers
in its fullness the meaning of life and the love of God. As he
comes to know God, he taps the font of all knowledge and
upon achieving union he finds that he shares fully in the
greatness and glory of God. Formerly an outcast and alien
to its own divinity, the soul at last knows beyond all doubt
that God is its essence and inheritance.

The entire drama of these cycles raises a question that at
one time or another plagues every serious religionist. Why
does God bother with these painful and arduous cycles of rebirth? There is something almost wantonly playful about a
God who would disperse himself throughout the phenomenal
world just for the pleasure of gathering himself in again.
The answer to this question solves the mystery of life itself,
and only those who have reached the end know. The paradox
is that he who penetrates the mystery finds that mere words
cannot convey it. For the present we must be content with
the answer that, had God not expressed himself, neither his
majesty nor his love would have been made known.

II

REINCARNATION
AND THE PERSONALITY

According to the theories proposed in the previous chapter, all the ingredients that constitute one's essential personality accumulate from one life to another. In the face of this supposition, many enigmatic aspects of personality and special aptitudes appear in a new light. Ordinarily we attribute many of our most important decisions—the choice of a partner in marriage or our profession—to the chance arrangements of fortune. Rarely do we give any further thought to the very strong attractions and repulsions that in fact determine our lives. We fall in love, we are irresistibly drawn to a certain calling, and with that the pattern of our life is set. If, however, our personality is seen as an accumulation from the past, rather than the chance stroke of fate or the inevitable product of environment, then the pattern of one's life emerges as the coherent sequel to the soul's millennial history.

Although this aspect of reincarnation has little to do with questions of theology, it does underscore the practical appeal of the belief. Specifically, the belief in reincarnation enlarges the perspective on personality and character from the confines of a single life to the limitless expanse of the ages.

Some writers have endeavored to prove reincarnation by pointing to strong character traits as vestiges from earlier lives. To do this is to advance a theory on the basis of wholly circumstantial evidence. Indeed, any "evidence" is of questionable value, for the doctrine of reincarnation is generally ac-

cepted as a matter of faith or intuition rather than a matter
of proof. The decision whether or not to assent to reincarnation is generally determined by very subtle aspects of one's
innermost predisposition. And yet, although I make no claims
for the material presented in this chapter as proof, I do hope
that it may influence those who are already predisposed in
favor of reincarnation. Those who are inclined to reject reincarnation, however, will find things in this chapter that are
very difficult to explain otherwise.

The category of so-called evidence most difficult to explain
is the many instances of confirmed recollections from previous lives. Until recently the outstanding case of this sort
concerned Shanti Devi, publicized in the year 1937. She
lived in Delhi in India and from the age of four she would
talk repeatedly about a former incarnation. She went so far
as to describe her previous home, and after some coaxing she
even gave the name of her husband from this avowed earlier
life. Shanti Devi's incredulous relatives wrote to the man at
the address given by her, and to their astonishment they received a reply confirming many details, including the demise
of his wife.

Finally she was taken from Delhi to Mattra, the town of
her supposed earlier life. Here she recognized many features
of the town and spoke of others as changed since she had
last seen them. Upon encountering an old Brahmin, she recognized him as her father-in-law of the alleged earlier life. One
of the most telling incidents of her story concerned a hoard of
money she claimed to have buried in a corner of her previous
home. The party that accompanied her from Delhi dug at
the designated place and recovered an empty cashbox. Later
the supposed husband of the earlier life admitted having removed the money after the passing of his wife.

One might object that this story took place in India, where
reincarnation is widely accepted, and that it was recorded
by Indian witnesses who lacked the skepticism of a Western
observer. Such objections have been very amply met, however,

by the recent work of Ian Stevenson of the Department of Neurology and Psychiatry at the Medical School of the University of Virginia. In a book entitled *Twenty Cases Suggestive of Reincarnation* (American Society for Psychical Research, New York, 1966), Dr. Stevenson gives the results of his painstaking and rigorous research. Those who are skeptical of the confessional and fervently attested statements of Indians will find in Dr. Stevenson a thoughtful and sober researcher. As the work unfolds, Dr. Stevenson never deviates from the posture of a scientist presenting data; he is not the apologist pleading a cherished belief. He has put the Western reader on reincarnation very much in his debt for his precise and thoughtful treatment of recollected lives.

His research extends to no fewer than six hundred cases, although only twenty appear in his book. His published material covers instances from India, Ceylon, Brazil, Alaska, and Lebanon. A summary of the first case he relates will give an idea of his method and findings.

In April of 1950 a boy of ten named Nirmal died in Kosi Kalan in the district of Mathura in India. In August of 1951 a boy named Prakash was born in the town of Chhatta, six miles distant from Kosi Kalan.

This Prakash was given to much crying in his early years and at the age of four and a half he used to run out of his home at night and say that his name was Nirmal and that he wanted to go home to Kosi Kalan. He made a number of these attempts and in 1956 prevailed upon his family to take him to Kosi Kalan. At this time he did not actually meet Nirmal's family. He continued, however, to have vivid recollections of his life as Nirmal, until Nirmal's family heard of his claims. In the summer of 1961 Nirmal's father happened to be in Chhatta on business and took time out to look up Prakash. Prakash recognized him at once as his former father. Nirmal's family made another visit to Chhatta and this time Prakash wept for joy upon seeing Tara, Nirmal's older sister. Nirmal's family asked the family of Prakash to allow the boy to go to

Kosi Kalan. They consented and many more startling feats of recognition were recorded.

Dr. Stevenson investigated the case in July of 1961 and spoke with no fewer than seventeen witnesses, among them the mother and father of the deceased Nirmal, the mother and father of Prakash, and Prakash himself. On the basis of these interviews Dr. Stevenson established thirty-four items of information. Here are some of the more striking ones that he was able to verify. Prakash recalled the names of the father, sister, and neighbors of Nirmal's family. He knew that Nirmal's father owned a grain shop, a cloth shop, and a general store. When he saw Nirmal's sister, Tara, for the first time, he recognized her and addressed her by name. There were many more details of people, streets, and personal effects that were correctly identified by Prakash during his visits to Kosi Kalan.

Such a body of information creates serious problems for the skeptic. In Dr. Stevenson's book one finds a massive accumulation of data which is very difficult to account for by any theory other than reincarnation. Repeatedly his subjects provided information to which they had no evident access. The possibility of fraud in such a large survey seems remote, especially since those interviewed did not stand to gain anything. Indeed, for some of them it was a considerable nuisance, and they were reluctant participants in Dr. Stevenson's research.

The peculiar interest of Dr. Stevenson's findings is that they shift the discussion from the theological to the purely practical dimension. By their very nature, theological questions stand in a remote and abstract relationship to life as it is experienced from day to day. Only rarely can the proponent of a theological assumption enlist empirical and pragmatic considerations in support of his argument. The case for reincarnation, however, does impinge upon some of the tangible realities of everyday life.

Incidental to Dr. Stevenson's research, many otherwise imponderable and enigmatic quirks of personality appear in a new light. For example, in the six hundred cases studied, he found that 10 percent of his subjects claimed a change of sex since their previous incarnation, and in many of these cases he observed that the subject had a wavering and ambiguous sense of sexual identity. Exceptionally strong bonds of affection also seemed to pass from one life to another. In some instances Dr. Stevenson's subjects found themselves very powerfully attracted to specific members of their previous family, and frequently such feelings were returned. Many of his subjects refused to leave the company of their newly found former families. The recognition was immediate and the attraction sometimes proved to be stronger than that which the subjects felt for their present families.

These discoveries of Dr. Stevenson open vast and intriguing vistas on the source and continuity of our deepest feelings. One of the great imponderables of love, for example—the power of spontaneous and irresistible attractions—is a little less mysterious when seen in the light of Dr. Stevenson's findings. So often people speak of love as finding themselves in the spell of a relationship that seems primordial and overpowering compared to all else. As Aristophanes says in Plato's *Symposium*, a lover who has found his beloved gives the appearance of one who has at last recovered that long-lost part of himself without which he must remain forever defective and incomplete. Although this experience of being smitten to the core of one's being does not necessarily suggest reincarnation to all, the great German poet Goethe read precisely this significance into his love for Charlotte von Stein. Here is a poem in which he celebrates the primeval force of attraction between them.

CHARLOTTE

Tell me what fate has planned for us.
How did it join us in such close accord?
In ages now gone by
You were my sister or my wife.

You knew the hidden recess of my being,
And of my soul you grasped the subtle resonance.
With just a glance you saw me to the core,
To depths unseen by any other eye.
You quelled the raging torrent in my veins,
My wild and erring course you set aright—
Until my heart, shattered and distraught,
Finally found its rest within your angel arms.

What Goethe senses here is the very thing reported by Dr. Stevenson's subjects—that powerful bond of affection which rides upon a deep current far beneath the surface of our lives. In such relationships there arise at once a directness of communication and a profundity of mutual understanding that seem to leap across time and space.

This aspect of love was also treated in a touching and uncharacteristically tender story by Mark Twain entitled "My Platonic Sweetheart." In this story he tells of a recurring dream of great vividness in which he found himself again and again loving the same girl in many different guises. This dream personage first intrudes upon Twain when he is in his late teens, and she revisits him on an average of every two years until he is in his sixties. In these dreams he is always seventeen and his beloved is always fifteen. All else changes, however: her appearance, her name, his name, and the setting are always different. In one such dream she expires in his arms in Hawaii. In another he is courting her amidst the grandeur of the Old South. In yet another he loves her in ancient Athens.

What he finds extraordinary about all these encounters is that whenever they meet, there is no sense of separation. In each new dream they meet and talk with the most simple and unabashed affection. Recognition is immediate, despite the changes of name and appearance. Although there has been the apparent separation of time and space, they love and understand each other as though they had never been apart. Twain does not assign these vivid encounters to the theory of reincarnation; like Goethe's experience, however, his are reminiscent of those overpowering and spontaneous attractions experienced by Dr. Stevenson's subjects upon meeting former loved ones. Where Dr. Stevenson's subjects, as well as Mark Twain and Goethe, converge is in the realization that the pull of affection can sometimes be so immediate and overpowering as to point almost irresistibly toward a source more profound and ancient than the events of a single lifetime. In all his dream encounters Twain finds it utterly touching that this experience of love is based upon a familiarity that cuts across time and space.

To venture to offer material such as Goethe's feelings about Charlotte or Twain's reflections on his "Platonic Sweetheart" as proof of reincarnation is to claim too much. These powerful first-sight reactions, however, do present a question to which the theory of reincarnation offers an especially attractive solution.

If all souls are evolving as they proceed from one life to another, it makes very good sense to assume that we shall indeed be thrown together with the same people again and again. One of the duties imposed upon man by the cycles of rebirth is to perfect himself through his relationships with others. Such evolution would be halting and sporadic if we had to start all our close relationships anew from one life to another. It is much more consistent with the progressive emphasis of reincarnation if we pick up the unfinished business of lives gone by. Thus brothers, sisters, parents, lovers, and close friends are figures from the past all returning to make right the wrong and perfect the good they have done to their fellowman. As Goethe intimates in his poem to Charlotte, the relationship may change from wife to sister to beloved; what remains constant is the bond—the sum of kindness and understanding that has gone before. Each life provides a unique opportunity to work out the complexities of the past on a new level. Again and again we meet those we have either loved or abused in the past, until at last there is a gradual leveling of all extremes of hate or attachment.

It is, in fact, quite logical to assume that the attractions and aversions that follow us from life to life extend beyond friends and family to everything that we do. Despite our cherished assumptions about free will, we often discover, at least in retrospect, that the major decisions in our lives have been determined by almost irresistible impulses. The man who is powerfully drawn to the clergy and enjoys a rewarding life in this calling realizes that nothing in the world would have made him become a real estate developer. The student who is powerfully drawn to the study of a certain language or culture cannot wholly account for the source of this attraction.

To the believer in reincarnation, however, there is nothing enigmatic about the choices and tendencies that finally shape our lives. Although the particulars of the past are forgotten, special inclinations and aptitudes belong to our *samskāras*— traces from past states of being that persist long after their cause is forgotten. Thus those who are powerfully drawn to certain languages, societies, and ages of the past are merely responding to traces from earlier lives. For the average man, unlike Dr. Stevenson's subjects, the memory fades; inclinations and aptitudes persist. The student who loathes French or Latin in school can perhaps comfort himself with the thought that his aversion is the result of unpleasant experiences, now long forgotten, with Frenchmen or Romans.

According to the reincarnationist, not only likes and dislikes persist but also exceptional aptitude. Hence reincarnation offers an attractive explanation of the child prodigy. When we apply the word "prodigy" to this phenomenon, we are simply declaring that these are freaks of nature not to be accounted for by known conventions. If, however, man progresses and grows from one life to another, what is called prodigious may be interpreted simply as the evidence of proficiency in earlier lives.

Mozart, whose life is well documented, can be taken as

a classic instance of the child prodigy. The following episodes, recorded by Andreas Schachter, a friend of the family, suggest the extraordinary extent of young Mozart's ability. One day Schachter and Mozart's father came into the house to find the four-year-old Mozart busy with pen and paper. They asked him what he was doing, and he announced that he was composing a piano concerto. Mozart's father, himself an accomplished musician, asked to see it. At first it appeared to be a jumble of smudges and blots. As he looked more closely, however, and tried to discover the music behind these marks, tears welled up in his eyes. As a composition it was not only technically correct but also extremely difficult. When Mozart's father commented on the difficulty of the piece, the boy explained that this was the very reason why he had composed it as a concerto, for it would require much practice.

On another occasion around the same time, Schachter was playing a string trio with Mozart's father and a third musician. The child Mozart asked to play the second violin and was of course refused, as he had never even had instruction in the violin. Undaunted, he answered that there was no need to study in order to play the second violin and proceeded to have a tantrum when he was again refused. They finally capitulated, but insisted that he play very softly so as not to disturb the performance. The man on the second violin suddenly realized that his contribution was quite superfluous and stopped entirely in order to listen to the rendition by the boy. Again Mozart's father was moved to tears.

To call such a person a child prodigy only describes; it does not begin to account for him. These instances of extraordinary talent are at best merely circumstantial evidence for reincarnation. Although they prove nothing about the soul or the cycle of rebirth, they do offer very provocative evidence that the human personality rests upon layers of experience and accumulated resources that we cannot otherwise explain. Many, in fact, are attracted to the belief in reincarnation because they dimly sense that the composite of their present personality surely must represent more than the meager experiences of a single life. Anyone who has engaged in serious introspection is aware of deep and disparate tendencies in his nature for which he can give no satisfactory account. For the reincarnationist, the enigma of man's personality is explained. What you are now is the composite of layer upon layer of experience—each disappearing from conscious memory but leaving its traces. All that we speak of as natural endowment is in fact the result of hard work: whatever unusual proficiency one may possess stands upon the concerted efforts of the past.

Indeed reincarnation can provide a satisfying account for many of the extremes and eccentricities of human character. Consider the case of irrational phobias—heights, water, confining rooms. If reincarnation is true, then the traces of many deaths are engraved upon the soul. Who can say how many drownings, suffocations, and grim mutilations lie in the distant past of each man?

Examples illustrating personality in terms of the soul's millennial journey can be multiplied almost indefinitely. What I have tried to indicate here are some of the more vivid aspects of personality that seem to suggest strong prenatal disposition. Yet this avenue of approach falls far short of disclosing the soul's career with any certainty. The history of the soul is known only to those who elude the oblivion that intervenes from life to life. For the rest, reincarnation must remain an unproved theory that may help to account for man's personality, but lacks the final confirmation of memory.

III

REINCARNATION
AND THE SELF

One of the most important features of any philosophy or religious system is the view that it takes of man, and these can range from the completely theistic to the completely secular. Seen within the perspective of the theistic view, man is a creature whose highest aspirations look beyond this world to a transcendent power acknowledged as the source of all being. In such a system the self is seen as both derived from and striving toward the eternal and perfect goodness of God. Secular man, however, acknowledges no transcendent source or goal to life and sees his self as a composite of physical, mental, and emotional needs that arise from his existence as an organism. Between these two extremes there, of course, lie countless possibilities.

The belief in reincarnation carries with it a distinctly theistic notion of what man's true nature is. The systems that have embraced reincarnation, whether Platonism or Hinduism, have seen in man an imperishable spark of the divine. The very center and core of his being, that everlasting essence which transmigrates from one life to another, is nothing less than a particle of God himself. This assumption about man, apparent to the convinced reincarnationist, has profound consequences for the believer's entire view of life.

First, this view is basically optimistic about man and his destiny, both here and beyond. If man is a particle of God, he can never be lost from God's sight. This means that the possibility of eternal damnation is removed. Secondly, the world and its experiences are seen as transient and unimportant when compared to the lasting and fixed nature of man. All the vicissitudes and tribulations of life dwindle to unimportance as man cognizes his true nature. What happens to the outer man is so much fretting on the stage of life, when compared with the unshakable divinity of the inner man. Thirdly, this view very naturally leads to the religion of mysticism. (By mysticism I mean taking specific measures to achieve direct inner communion with God.) Fourthly, the goal of the religious life is God-realization. That is to say, the traditional Christian looks forward to being adopted into the Kingdom of God, whereas the reincarnationist, confident of his own latent divinity, strives to arouse full consciousness of this. Once he has merged his conciousness with the Absolute, he can say that he has reached his goal. At this point every distinction between subject and object, lover and beloved, vanishes, and the divine drop of the soul consciously rides upon the great swell of Spirit.

The traditional Christian view of man, no less theistic than that of the reincarnationist, would differ on all four points mentioned above. This divergence arises out of conflicting views about man's source. Where the reincarnationist insists that man's innermost essence is a part of God himself, the traditional Christian places man at a considerable distance from God. Mankind, rather than being so many fragments of God, is viewed as the creature of God. This is a very significant difference, for implicit in the act of creation is separation and distinction between creature and creator. Traditional Christianity makes this separation quite explicit, for man, although made in the image and likeness of God (Gen. 1:26), is created from the dust of the earth (Gen. 2:7). As for the earth, it was created *ex nihilo*, from the void. This means that when man looks back to his source he discovers that he is partially estranged from God, for the relationship is not the direct and consubstantial one that exists between the sun and its rays, but is rather the oblique and precarious position of a suppliant. Here are some of the major consequences for the religious life that arise from these conflicting views of the self.

The Threat of Damnation

One of the most attractive aspects of reincarnation is that it removes entirely the possibility of damnation. For man to be either saved or damned, he must be to some extent separate and estranged from God. Any doctrine of salvation and damnation will have this assumption as its foundation. Consider, for example, this statement from Augustine on the nature of man.

> God placed man's nature between that of the beasts and the angels, so that if man were submissive to his Creator and observed his commandments in pious obedience, he would enter into the company of angels and attain eternal life free from the intervention of death. If, however, man should offend the Lord God by making arrogant and disobedient use of his free will, he will be given over to death to live as a beast, as the slave of his passions, and destined to eternal punishment after death. (*City of God* 12.22.)

Augustine envisions man here as a lonely and isolated creature, balanced precariously between the gates of heaven and the abyss of hell. He has no claims upon the Kingdom of Heaven and must await to be judged on his feeble merits. God would of course prefer to see him go to heaven and sends forth his grace to make this the more attractive choice. Nonetheless, man cannot claim any right to heaven on the basis of kinship with God. God has created him at such a distance from himself that, although God may perhaps agree to adopt man, man has no claims upon God's special favor. One should hasten to add, in defense of Augustine and his views upon man's fallen nature, that the more fallen man is, the more

God's grace is magnified. Stated in its most extreme form, this view concedes no merit to man and all merit to God, who will finally uplift his undeserving creature.

Such a theology is only meaningful, however, with the dramatic contrast provided by a vivid doctrine of damnation. To preach salvation is by definition to preach damnation, for deliverance is meaningless unless there is some very palpable threat to be delivered from. Thus theologians conjure up visions of damnation wherein God allows man's soul to fall irredeemably and forever from his sight.

This raises a delicate theological problem: How does God, who is all-powerful and all-pervasive, create something that does not fully partake of his nature? If man is fully the creature of God, one would assume that he has the attributes of God. We would like to think that man, God's creature, shares in his immortality, power, and felicity. This, however, does not prove to be the case. Here is how Augustine accounts for the origin of a creature that does not partake of its Creator:

> That which is of Him must of necessity be of His nature and, as a result, must be immutable. Everyone agrees, however, that the soul is mutable. Thus it cannot be of Him; for it is not immutable, as He is. If, however, it is created from no substance, then without doubt it is created from nothing, although by Him. (*On the Soul and Its Origin* 1.4.4.)

Not only does man stand orphaned before God, but he comes from the void. Seen in this light, man has no ancestry, no past, and no claims upon the future. He stands as a wretched and fallen creature of the great void and only by the goodness of God can he hope for any assurance about the future. Given this view of man's nature, salvation and damnation are very real possibilities. Thus salvation means that man is adopted from the void into the fullness of God's eternal Kingdom, and damnation means that he does not make the grade and remains eternally estranged from God.

This is a view which some Christians find difficult to accept, for it raises questions about the limits of God's love. It means that God fashions creatures out of the void, gives them free will, only to turn his back on some of them in the end. This is abhorrent to anyone who sees God's love as perfect and all-embracing. Although the fundamentalists still preach eternal damnation, more liberal Christianity is moving toward a view in which God's forgiveness will finally take in all creatures.

To those who find eternal damnation degrading, both to man and to God, the reincarnationist view of the Self is much more attractive. Here is a typical statement from India:

> Finite are these bodies, but the occupant, they say, is eternal, indestructible, and cannot be measured. Whoever thinks that the Self can inflict death or that it can suffer death—both are mistaken; for the Self neither kills nor is killed. It is not born, it does not die. Never has it come into being, nor will it be born again. The Self is unborn, eternal, everlasting; nor does it die when the body dies. (*Bhagavad-Gita* 2.18–20.)

These words spoken by Krishna, an incarnation of the Godhead, proclaim, not just that the death of the body is a mere transition, but also that the soul itself is so constituted that it cannot suffer any of the vicissitudes of the phenomenal world. That the soul could undergo any such final and devastating transition as separation from God is unthinkable here. Not only is the soul birthless and deathless, it is also divine. Here again are the words of Krishna:

> An eternal part of myself, having become a living entity in the world of living things, draws to itself the five senses and the mind as a sixth—all of them fixed in the world of nature. (*Bhagavad-Gita* 15.7.)

What is significant here is the divinity of the soul and the fact that all else—mind and senses—is incidental. Krishna gives man much to hope for, since man stands before God, not as a beggar, but rather as a prodigal son who has momentarily lost his way in creation. There is no such thing as either salvation or damnation, for God cannot cast away that which is in fact a part of himself.

Passages can be found in Plato that develop the same theme:

> "Consider this," said Socrates. "On the basis of what has been said, it can be maintained that the soul is most similar to that which is divine, immortal, intelligible, uniform, indestructible, and ever-abiding, fixed in itself. The body, on the contrary, is most similar to that which is human, mortal, multiform, beneath intellect, corruptible, and never abiding fixed in itself." (*Phaedo* 80B.)

Here again the phenomenal world and the divine world are juxtaposed. Man, whose true abode is the divine world, makes contact with the phenomenal world only through the body, which is itself mortal, whereas man's true nature is spirit and his true home is with the divine. Man as viewed from this perspective needs neither to call out for salvation nor to fear damnation. He is now, always has been, and ever will be a member of God's Kingdom. For the man who sees himself in this way, the threat of hell is meaningless.

The Dream of Worldly Life

A second assumption that naturally follows from the reincarnationist view is that all the trials and tribulations we suffer in this world are of little consequence. If the essence and nature of the soul is pure, unchanging divinity, then, like God himself, it cannot be affected by that which it experiences through the body. All of its experiences, in fact, are no more than scenes and vignettes that come and go while the soul is sojourning in forgetfulness of its true nature.

Here again both Hinduism and Platonism are in accord. One of the most vivid and best-known descriptions of life's dreamlike quality is found in Plato's allegory of the cave (*Republic* 514–516), where he describes the experiences of an unenlightened man as no more than the play of light and shadow on the back of a cave. Men think that these shadows are real, but in fact they are just projected from cutout silhouettes, which are themselves copies of reality. Thus the average man passes his life in a deluded state, taking the remote reflection of things as their very reality.

The Hindus describe this deception of man with the term *māyā*, which is a spell or charm that God casts upon the world in such a way as to beguile men and create the appearance of "reality." Unenlightened man, therefore, is no better than a dreamer, for he sees this vast interplay of God's energy as solid and enduring objects that can have a lasting and significant effect upon him.

Conventional Christianity is often uncomfortable in the presence of any view that exalts the transcendent and spiritual while downgrading physical creation. If God is the author of creation and found it wholly good at the end of the sixth day, who are we to stratify things, saying that the physical world is a deceptive magic lantern show that simply holds men in bondage, when in the eyes of God everything is a seamless and perfect whole?

In fact, both Hindu and Platonist would agree that the world is wholly good. The allegory of the cave and the spell of *māyā* are devices for describing man's deception, not for passing judgment on creation. For the reincarnationist, man's greatest problem and the source of all his ills lies in the fact that he attaches absolute importance to things that are, in fact, of only relative consequence. The man who sinks into profound depression over some financial setback is making the mistake of thinking that his innermost and essential self is affected, whereas in actuality what is affected is only the outer composite of name, wage earner, mortgage holder, and the many other incidentals that determine our place in the world.

To tell a person that despondency over material loss is delusion does not in any way devaluate this world. It is simply a way of saying that the man has a mistaken notion of where his true interest lies. His real Self is neither name, wage earner, nor mortgage holder: it is an imperishable spark of the divine that looks upon success and failure with the carefree dispassion of a spectator.

This world, in fact, possesses a very compelling reality to the extent that it is the proving ground of the soul. As mentioned in the discussion of *karma*, action is the law of life. Although man needs the world to discover and assert his spirituality, his origin and essence are not of this world.

The Religion of the Mystic

A third consequence of the reincarnationist view is to cultivate the soul and seek out experiences in which the body does not share. The view of man's self as divine very naturally leads to a mystical approach to religion. By mystical I mean following any course of action that leads to direct interior communion with God, as contrasted with good works, ritual, and ceremony, which affirm God's goodness, majesty, and love but do not necessarily bestow inner glimpses of him.

This is not to say that conventional Christianity does not offer anything for the mystic. Although there have always been Christian mystics, the more typical attitude of the Christian is found in the passage: "For since the creation of the world his invisible attributes are clearly seen—his everlasting power also and divinity—being understood through things that are made" (Rom. 1:20). For the great majority of Christians the attempt to experience or know God finds adequate fulfillment "through things that are made." That is to say, whatever need an individual may have to savor God's nature can be gratified by performing charitable works, witnessing, preaching the Word and many other activities that are aimed at the outer world.

I do not mean to minimize these activities, for they are absolutely essential ingredients of the religious life—as much for the mystic as for anyone else. Every serious religionist discovers that intimations of God's presence are to be found in the midst of "things that are made": what distinguishes the mystic, however, is that he endeavors to discover intimations of God's presence independent of "things that are made."

It is at the threshold between "things that are made" and what lies beyond that the life of the mystic starts. For the traditional Christian, however, there may be some doubt as to the direction of the mystic's quest; for the reincarnationist this presents no problem, for he believes that at the core of his own being lies God himself. The traditional Christian, who sees man as no more than animated dust of the earth, cannot be so confident about the goal of the inward journey. Consider, for example, the following passage from Augustine:

> When did I find truth, when did I find my God, who is truth itself? From the moment I learned of you, I never forgot. Thus, since the time I learned of you, you abide in my memory and there I find you when I think back on you and delight in you. . . . And where did I find you, that I might learn of you? For you were not in my memory before I learned of you. When did I find you, that I might learn of you, if not in you and above me? (*Confessions* 10.25–26.)

This passage is mystical to the extent that it speaks of the inner quest for God. It diverges from the reincarnationist view, however, to the extent that God is not experienced as man's native essence. Augustine takes delight in being with God in recollection, but he is fully aware that at one time God was extraneous to him. Only after God has reached down and left traces of his sweetness in the memory of man can any sort of reflective communion take place.

For the reincarnationist, however, there can be no question that the mystic path leads within and that God is to be found at the core of man's being. Communion then takes place, not through the memory, which is merely an aspect of the mind's self-contemplation, but within the sacred Self. Leaving behind "things that are made" as well as the limited faculties of mind and senses, the Self comes face to face with the Lord. Here is an excellent example of this experience from the sacred literature of India.

> He who finds joy in the Self, with his Self beyond all sense contact, this one, united with the Lord through spiritual exertion, attains undying joy. (*Bhagavad-Gita* 5.21.)

The "Self" spoken of here is the Atman, the Sanskrit word for the spark of divinity that comprises the very core and essence of the individual. What is important here is that the mystical moment is not seen as God reaching down from above to touch a creature previously estranged from him. Rather, it is a matter of cutting through everything that intrudes from the created world and realizing deep within the unity between one's own divine spark and the infinite fire which emits that spark.

It is for this reason that religious systems sympathetic to reincarnation so often advocate introspective practices. The point of these practices, whether it is the Yoga of India or the contemplation of the Neoplatonists, is to withdraw from the impressions of the senses, so that one may realize the latent divinity within. At the same time, I certainly do not wish to imply that Christianity has been without mystics; men are subject to the mystic impulse regardless of creed and culture. The first Christian contemplative could probably be said to be Mary (Luke 10:38–42), who imbibed the presence of Jesus while her sister Martha busied herself with serving the needs of the Lord. From Anthony in the desert to the nameless author of *The Way of the Pilgrim*, there have been

Christians who turned their back on the world in order to find God. The fact remains, however, that such men are the isolated exceptions rather than the norm in Christianity.

Union: The Goal of Religion

A fourth consequence of the reincarnationist view of the Self involves a somewhat different goal of religious life from that proposed by traditional Christianity. For the Christian, the culmination of the religious life is salvation, which means that the soul has been rescued forever from any danger of falling from God's sight and has been adopted into the Kingdom of God. There man will be resurrected in a perfect and incorruptible body through which he will have an unbroken vision of God's majesty. Here is how Augustine envisioned the redeemed Christian in his resurrected body:

> What a body it will be!—subject to the spirit in every way and so sustained by spirit that it will never need nourishment. Nor will this body belong to animal creation. It will be spiritual, possessing to be sure the substance of flesh, but free from the corruption of flesh. (*City of God* 22.24.)

The first and most important thing ensured by salvation is that one is free from death, for, until this time, man's state in eternity hangs in doubt. The second and culminating feature of Christian salvation is the beatific vision. Here is Augustine again:

> Therefore it is perfectly possible and credible that we shall view physical bodies of the new earth and the new heaven in such a way that, wherever we look, we shall behold God with the utmost clarity, everywhere present and presiding over all things. We shall experience this through our new bodies and the things that we see. Nor will we see the invisible attributes of God as we do now, through the things that are made, seen, and understood but in part and as through a glass darkly. (*City of God* 22.29.)

Here man neither merges with God nor achieves union. The subject-object relationship is maintained eternally. There may be a great and deep sense of communion, but the creature is forever different and apart from his Creator. The best that man can hope for is to look upon God; to merge would be blasphemy.

Again the systems that embrace reincarnation have a different view of the consummation of religion. The ultimate experience of the religious life for them is *samādhi, unio mystica*, i.e., the complete dissolution of the subject-object relationship and the absorption of man's spirit back into its divine source. If man is indeed a spark of God, then the natural goal of the religious life is for this spark to know beyond all doubt its identity with its primal sacred source. Patanjali, the great exponent of Yoga, describes this experience in a typically terse but illuminating sutra.

One who has stilled the motions of the mind, just like a noble gem, he plunges into that state where the viewer, the object viewed, and the act of viewing merge. (*Yoga Sutras* 1.41.)

The state itself of necessity defies description. The simile of the noble gem is very helpful, however, for there is in a perfect gem translucence within, luster without, and an awesome and absolute self-sufficiency. When the Self becomes fully integrated with its sustaining principle, there is a unity of function, action, and essence that leaves behind all description. Such is the state of one who has united his own soul with the divine.

The fact that such a view does not accord with traditional Christianity is sadly illustrated by the fate of the medieval German mystic, Meister Eckhart. In the year 1329 he was condemned by Pope John XXII and among the articles of his condemnation was the following:

The Father created me as his Son, and the Same Son. Whatever God accomplishes is one. For this reason he created me as his Son, without distinction. (*Errors of Eckhart* 22.)

REINCARNATION AND THE SELF

For reasons that readers of the foregoing material from Augustine can appreciate, the church was constrained to take exception to a man who presumed to equate himself with the Son "without distinction." When speaking of the moment of mystical union, Eckhart uses language that would be thoroughly acceptable to the reincarnationist.

> We are transformed entirely into God and converted into him, just as the bread in the Sacrament is converted into the body of Christ. Thus I am transformed into him, for he works upon me as his own, not as something similar. By the living God, this is true, for there is no distinction. (*Errors of Eckhart* 10.)

Here is a vivid and powerful statement from a practicing mystic who, in his moments of deepest interiorization, found that man and God are no different. In the face of such an experience the history of dogma has no influence.

There have always been Christians who were inclined to believe in man's essential divinity and the need for the inward quest. They can point to Biblical passages such as "Behold, the kingdom of God is within you" (Luke 17:21), or "Be still, and know that I am God" (Ps. 46:10), or "I have said: You are gods and all of you sons of the Most High" (Ps. 82: 6). Perhaps now that Christianity is no longer so bound by a sense of tradition, mysticism may gain some momentum. Should this be the case, Christians will be looking with greater sympathy and understanding to the assumption common in the East and once common in the West that man carries deep within himself a germ of the divine.

IV

REINCARNATION
AND THE CHURCH

The Christian church has never explicitly come to terms with
the doctrine of reincarnation. It is only by inference from the
controversies about resurrection, the nature of the soul, and
the nature of salvation that one perceives a system of thought
that is generally hostile to this belief. If, however, the same
ingenuity were devoted to reincarnation as to such beliefs as
the consubstantiality of the Trinity or the virgin birth, reincarnation could readily be brought into harmony with the
main body of Christian thought.

During the period from A.D. 250 to 553 controversy raged,
at least intermittently, around the name of Origen, and from
this controversy emerged the major objections that orthodox
Christianity might raise against reincarnation. A close study
of these objections will show the Christian who is inclined
toward reincarnation what implications this belief has and
how he may answer critics from within the church. What
one discovers from such a study is that it is perfectly possible
for the reincarnationist to accept personal salvation through
Jesus Christ as the only-begotten Son of God. Such, after all,
was the belief of one of Christianity's greatest systematic theologians, Origen of Alexandria—who was also a believer in
reincarnation.

Origen was a man devoted to Scriptural authority, a scourge
to the enemies of the church, and a martyr for the faith. He
was the spiritual teacher of a large and grateful posterity and
yet was anathematized in 553. The debates and controversies

that flared up around his teachings are in fact the record of reincarnation in the church. Although the controversy did not deal directly with the belief in reincarnation, anyone who familiarizes himself with this debate will know what objections to expect from orthodoxy and some possible answers against them.

The case against Origen grew by fits and starts from about A.D. 300 (fifty years after his death) until 553. There were writers of great eminence among his critics as well as some rather obscure ecclesiasts. They included Methodius of Olympus, Epiphanius of Salamis, Theophilus, Bishop of Jerusalem, Jerome, and the Emperor Justinian. The first of these, Methodius of Olympus, was a bishop in Greece and died a martyr's death in the year 311. He and Peter of Alexandria, whose works are almost entirely lost, represent the first wave of anti-Origenism. They were concerned chiefly with the preexistence of souls and Origen's notions about the resurrection of the dead. Another more powerful current against Origenism arose about a century later. The principals were Epiphanius of Salamis, Theophilus of Alexandria, and Jerome. From about 395 to 403 Origen became the subject of heated debate throughout Christendom. These three ecclesiasts applied much energy and thought in search of questionable doctrine in Origen. Again the controversy flared up around 535, and in the wake of this the Emperor Justinian composed a tract against Origen in 543, proposing nine anathemas against *On First Principles,* Origen's chief theological work. Origen was finally officially condemned in the Second Council of Constantinople in 553, when fifteen anathemas were charged against him.

The critics of Origen attacked him on individual points, and thus did not create a systematic theology to oppose him. Nonetheless, one can glean from their writings five major points that Christianity has raised against reincarnation:

1. It seems to minimize Christian salvation.
2. It is in conflict with the resurrection of the body.
3. It creates an unnatural separation between body and soul.

4. It is built on a much too speculative use of Christian Scriptures.
5. There is no recollection of previous lives.

Any discussion of these points will be greatly clarified by a preliminary look at Origen's system. Although it is of course impossible to do justice in a few pages to a thinker as subtle and profound as Origen, some of the distinctive aspects of his thought can be summarized along with the bare bones of a biography.

Origen's Life and Background

Origen was born in Alexandria of Christian parents in 184 or 185. Like any learned Greek or Roman of his era, he was educated in pagan literature. He was especially well versed in Platonism and, in fact, studied at one time under Ammonius Saccas, the father of Neoplatonism. His brilliance must have been apparent at an early age, for he became instructor of catechumens in Alexandria at the age of eighteen, succeeding Clement of Alexandria in the catechetical school. He evidently had a single-minded and austere nature, for he felt inspired to put into action the words of Matt. 19:12: "There are eunuchs who have made themselves so for the sake of the kingdom of heaven. Let him accept it who can." Origen accepted it and won more notoriety than credit with posterity by emasculating himself. He was always a teacher, spending the first portion of his life in Alexandria (203–231) and the remainder in Caesarea in Palestine. He also found time to travel widely, visiting Rome, Athens, and Arabia. During the persecutions of the Emperor Decius (250) he was cast into a dungeon and subjected to torture. He died in 253, probably as the indirect result of his imprisonment.

Although he met with more than his share of antagonism, especially in his native Alexandria, his popularity and influence were enormous. He wrote voluminously, composing a systematic theology, tracts on prayer and martyrdom, a defense of Christianity against the pagan critic Celsus, as well as numerous homilies and Scriptural commentaries. The fact that he was such a controversial figure in the church led to his works being suppressed by his opponents and altered into more orthodox form by his supporters. This is especially true of *On First Principles*, his most important work and one of the few major attempts of early Christianity at a systematic theology. Although originally composed in Greek, this work survives largely in the Latin version of Rufinus, a devoted admirer of Origen who did not hesitate to improve the orthodoxy of the master's work where he feared it might give offense.

It is quite apparent that Origen's system is scrupulously based on sacred Scripture, and yet the trend and coloring of Platonic thought prevails throughout. Platonic philosophy had firmly established itself in Alexandria about four hundred years before Origen's time, and anyone educated there was inevitably steeped in this tradition. Probably the most important doctrine of Platonism to influence Origen concerned the relationship between the body and the soul. Plato had proposed the theory that the soul, being divine and eternal, is inherently superior to the body, which, being physical matter, is subject to corruption. For a number of reasons, which vary within his works, Plato suggests that the soul is forcibly cast into the body, where it either prevails according to its own natural reason or is overwhelmed by the intemperance of the body.

The soul passes from one body to another until it has proven itself superior to the inclinations of the flesh. Then after many lives, or few if one had the good sense to be a philosopher, the soul wins freedom from the demands of the brutish and lustful body and is at liberty to return to its divine home under no compulsion to incarnate again. There are two features of this system which, as we shall see, have important implications for the Christian. First, the soul is viewed as a

divine and taintless essence that exists eternally, while the
body is corrupt and of short duration. Second, the soul needs
more than one incarnation to acquire the experience and lessons that will reconcile it with the Absolute.

When Origen set himself the task of creating a theology,
he did not have the explicit purpose of combining Plato with
the Scriptures. What he wished to do was to create a reasoned
system in which the origin, course, and goal of life under God
is accounted for. There was, for Origen, only one authority in
this: Holy Scripture. What he strove to do to the best of
his ability was to create a new system that was both free from
internal contradiction and consistent with Scripture. The
problem for anyone embarking on such a venture, as Augustine, Aquinas, and others were to discover, is that the Scriptures in fact do not supply the consistent, explicit, and complete information with which to build such a system. Many
areas, such as the prenatal and postmortem life of the individual, are only hinted at in the most vague and metaphorical
terms. Accordingly, the theologian either must eliminate certain topics from his inquiry or must venture forth into the
unknown with the utmost care and circumspection lest he
suggest something that might lead to heresy.

Here stands the choice of whether to dare speculative
thought. In the case of Augustine the risk was deemed too
great, and one sees him again and again retreating with re-
gret from areas where the Scriptures cannot light the way.
Origen, however, a Greek and a philosopher, was quite willing
to run the risk. Filling in the gaps with the Platonic philosophy that he knew from his education in Alexandria, he was
painstakingly cautious, and it took the most subtle thinkers
of the church three hundred years to find fault with what he
had created. He worked in good conscience, he prayed for
divine guidance, he was eminently imaginative, and he wrote
a work that he believed to be free from heresy.

Origen's Theology

Looking at the sequence of creation from its inception to its conclusion, one could summarize his system as follows: Originally all beings existed as pure mind on an ideational or thought level. Humans, angels, and heavenly bodies lacked incarnate existence and had their being only as ideas. This is a very natural view for anyone trained in both Christian and Platonic thought. Since there is no account in the Scriptures of what preceded creation, it seemed perfectly natural to Origen to appeal to Plato for his answers. That this could be injudicious or detrimental to orthodoxy hardly troubled him, nor did he think of Augustine's grim suggestion that before fashioning the world God was busy preparing a place of punishment for those with the audacity to speculate on what preceded creation.

God for the Platonist is pure intelligence and all things were reconciled with God before creation—an assumption which Scripture does not appear to contradict. Then as the process of fall began, individual beings became weary of their union with God and chose to defect or grow cold in their divine ardor. As the mind became cool toward God, it made the first step down in its fall and became soul. The soul, now already one remove from its original state, continued with its defection to the point of taking on a body. This, as we know from Platonism, is indeed a degradation, for the highest type of manifestation is on the mental level and the lowest is on the physical.

Such an account of man's fall does not mean that Origen rejected Genesis. It only means that he was willing to allow for allegorical interpretation; thus Eden is not necessarily spacially located, but is a cosmic and metaphysical event wherein pure disincarnate idea became fettered to physical matter. What was essential for Christianity, as Origen perceived, is that the fall be voluntary and result in a degree of estrangement from God.

Where there is a fall, there must follow the drama of conciliation. Love is one of God's qualities, as Origen himself
acknowledged, and from this it follows that God will take
an interest in the redemption of his creatures. For Origen
this means that after the drama of incarnation the soul assumes
once again its identity as mind and recovers its ardor for God.

It was to hasten this evolution that in the fullness of time
God sent the Christ. The Christ of Origen was the Incarnate
Word (he was also the only being that did not grow cold toward God), and he came both as a mediator and as an incarnate image of God's goodness. By allowing the wisdom and
light of God to shine in one's life through the inspiration of
Jesus Christ, the individual soul could swiftly regain its ardor
for God, leave behind the burden of the body, and regain
complete conciliation with God. In fact, said Origen, much to
the outrage of his critics, the extent and power of God's love
is so great that eventually all things will be restored to him,
even Satan and his legions.

Since the soul's tenancy of any given body is but one of many
episodes in its journey from God and back again, the doctrine
of reincarnation is implicit. As for the resurrection of the body,
Origen created a tempest of controversy by insisting that the
physical body wastes away and returns to dust, while the
resurrection takes on a spiritual or transformed body. This is
of course handy for the reincarnationist, for it means that the
resurrected body either can be the summation and climax of
all the physical bodies that came before or indeed may bear
no resemblance at all to the many physical bodies.

There will come a time when the great defection from God
that initiated physical creation will come to an end. All things,
both heavenly bodies and human souls, will be so pure and
ardent in their love for God that physical existence will no
longer be necessary. The entire cohesion of creation will come
apart, for matter will be superfluous. Then, to cite one of
Origen's favorite passages, all things will be made subject to
God and God will be "all in all." (I Cor. 15:28.) This restora-

tion of all things proposed by Origen gave offense in later centuries. It seemed quite sensible to Origen that anything that defects from God must eventually be brought back to him. As he triumphantly affirmed at the end of his *On First Principles,* men are the "blood brothers" of God himself and cannot stay away forever.

Here in a very compressed and simplified statement is a theology that acknowledges the fall of man, the power of God's grace, the mediation of Jesus Christ, and the resurrection of the dead. It covers the entire course of cosmic history from before the creation until after the dissolution. It accounts not only for man's sojourn here on earth but also for his existence before the worlds began and after they shall pass away. It is an edifice that is massively supported by citations from Scripture. The only flaw in the eyes of posterity lay in the fact that when Scripture could not answer Origen's needs, he borrowed heavily from Platonism to supplement his structure.

The Need for a Savior

With this sketch of Origenism before us, we can now consider the objections to reincarnation mentioned at the beginning of this chapter. One of the most powerful complaints that orthodoxy has to make about reincarnation is that it minimizes the salvific role of Jesus Christ. Here is an excerpt from a paschal letter of the year 402 by Theophilus, patriarch of Alexandria:

What is the point of preaching that souls are repeatedly confined in bodies, only to be released again, and that we experience many deaths? Does he [Origen] not know that Christ came, not in order to free souls from bodies after their resurrection or to clothe freed souls once again in bodies that they might come down from heavenly regions to be invested once again with flesh and blood? Rather, he came so that he might present our revived bodies with incorruptibility and eternal life. (Jerome, *Letters* 98.11.)

The important point brought out by this criticism is that the work of Christ is trivialized if man does not come to conciliation with God in one life. The penalty that Christ paid on the cross for all mankind is apparently insufficient if man needs several lives to be cleansed of sin. According to traditional orthodoxy, even though man has fallen short of his goal at the end of his life, Christ will make up the difference and present man, perfect in body and soul, before God. Thus man takes a few faltering steps toward conciliation with the Father, and then the Son intervenes and carries him the rest of the way.

Every Christian, whether orthodox or Origenist, recognizes that man has fallen from God. For Origen and the reincarnationist, however, since man fell from God of his own free will, he must also win his way back to God by his own efforts. This does not mean that God remains indifferent and remote. His grace is still at work and he sends his Son to light the way and make the reality of redemption more palpable and attractive. Christ is indeed a savior inasmuch as by the example and inspiration of his life he shows man that the longed-for goal is attainable. Nor need the suffering of Jesus be minimized, for he deliberately underwent crucifixion in order to carry out his ministry. If one is to speak of insufficiency, it is in man rather than in Christ. The life and ministry of Jesus Christ was perfect in every way, but the capacity of man to act upon it is limited.

The essential difference between Theophilus and Origen is this: For Origen, man, the creature of free choice, stands responsible before God for his initial defection. God uses all his love and persuasion to hasten man along his way, but man must go the whole journey. For Theophilus, however, part of the responsibility for man's defection from God is lifted from his shoulders by the Son. Thus man is a completely free and sovereign agent only when he falls; when he rises, however, much of the travail is being borne by another. Man does what he can in a single life and Christ will make good the rest.

This is one of the most significant objections that orthodoxy has to make against the belief in reincarnation. Reincarnation should be understood, however, not as a statement on Christ, but as a statement on man. Theophilus is in effect charging that man is so feeble that he must depend on Christ to take him most of the way. The reincarnationist, however, is convinced of man's divinity and hence of his innate ability to return to God's favor. Whether a man follows the path of discipleship for one life or many lives, Christ is no less the object of worship. Nowhere are the goodness and love of God more conspicuously visible than in the life of Christ. What greater inspiration for the man who may look forward to many lives before he returns to his heavenly abode? For the Christian reincarnationist, Christ lights the way and lightens the load right to the end.

Admittedly the role of Christ is somewhat different, but so is the role of man. Thanks to his Platonic background, Origen very frequently had his eye on the cosmic scope of things rather than on just the smaller secular drama. He saw defection from God at one end of time and reunion with God at the other end. In a manner typical of classical rather than Christian thought, he saw man's lonely and inescapable responsibility before the cosmos. Also typical of classical rather than Christian thought, he concedes to man the self-reliance and self-determination to traverse the entire stage from the beginning of time to the end.

Theophilus raises another related objection against Origen. Not only does Origen seem to minimize Christ's ministry by granting man many incarnations but he appears to minimize it even further by allowing that Christ could undergo several incarnations. Origen suggests that the redemptive power of the Son should be made available wherever necessary. Thus

Christ might well incarnate and undergo the passion amidst the realms of the demons, or indeed anyplace where there is apostasy from God. In short, it seemed reasonable to Origen that Christ would not limit his ministry simply to the men of this world. Theophilus takes offense at this (Jerome, *Letters* 92.5) and quotes Rom. 6:9–10: "Christ, having risen from the dead, dies no more; death shall no longer have dominion over him. For the death that he died, he died to sin for all, but the life that he lives, he lives unto God." As applied by Theophilus, this passage proclaims a rather grim finality for the Christian dispensation. Christ's life and passion comprise an utterly unique historical event, and all ages and men— past, present, and future—must look to this single isolated instance of God's goodness for guidance and salvation. The implications of this have not escaped science-fiction writers, who have mused over the prospect of salvation for the inhabitants of other planets.

Origen, however, always with an eye toward the cosmic drama, found it perfectly plausible that the Son of God would carry on his work wherever there was work to be done. This is important for the reincarnationist, for it offers a much-expanded view of Christ. For Origen, the emphasis was always more on the cosmic Word that is eternally occupied with the redemption of man than upon the historical and incarnate Jesus. This is, of course, very natural for the believer in reincarnation, whose eye is trained much more upon the long-range drama of redemption than upon the individual moment of accepting or rejecting Christ.

At the opposite extreme of the reincarnationist stands the revival-meeting preacher, who tells his listeners that at this very moment their soul rests on the balance between heaven and hell. Make the choice for redemption or writhe forever in the sulfurous fires. Although all recognize the importance of such turning points in one's life, both Origen and the reincarnationist would say that God would never bring one of his own to such a moment of final crisis, but rather makes his help available again and again until the job is done.

The Resurrection of the Body

Resurrection has long been a troublesome matter within Christian dogma and raises questions that have vexed the church for centuries. There have been debates over whether the resurrected body is of earthly flesh or of transfigured substance; whether a Catholic should be cremated; what happens when the body of the deceased is mutilated. In fact, current doctrine about resurrection has benefited enormously from the Origenist controversies.

When Origen's opponents affirmed the resurrection of the body, they took it for granted that the very body in which one had lived on earth was to be restored. Otherwise, they declared, resurrection would be meaningless. Here are the words of Epiphanius of Salamis:

> First of all if, as the Origenists say, another body succeeds this one, then the judgment of God is not just, for he will either be condemning the new body for the sins of the former one, or he will be ushering it into its glorious and heavenly inheritance in recognition of the fastings, vigils, and persecution suffered for the name of God by an earlier body. (Epiphanius, *Ancoratus* 87.)

Again one sees in this passage the inclination of traditional Christianity to assign fixed and permanent existence to the things of this world. The reincarnationist sees the things of this world as dim phantoms when compared to God's absolute existence. For orthodoxy, the Genesis account of creation suggests that the lasting stamp of God's blessing is embossed upon all that he made. Thus whatever was found good in creation will endure. The flesh will pass away only insofar as it defects from God. The things that God has sanctified, however, have a permanence no different from that of pure spirit. Babylon, like the corrupt flesh, will pass away, but the earthly Jerusalem shall become the Heavenly Jerusalem. According to orthodoxy, it is also thus with the body: the body was created by God and hence bears the lasting stamp of his blessing.

In Origen's view of these matters his Platonic background is apparent. He sees this world and the physical bodies that populate it as a lower and fallen order of existence. The physical objects to which men attribute reality are no more than the very gross projection of an ideational image or idea of the thing in question. Hence for the Platonist, all of material creation is viewed as the crude representation of pure form. This notion extends of course to the body, which the Platonist deplores as the adversary and corrupter of the taintless soul. For the Platonic philosopher, as for Origen, the entire goal of life is to disentangle the soul from the pernicious influence of the body. This stands in strong contrast to the statement of Epiphanius that the body is itself a living principle and whatever it has endured, it will carry before God for judgment.

Although Origen could conceive of a sequence of many bodies, he knew his Scriptures well enough to realize that a resurrection of some sort takes place. He took his inspiration from I Cor. 15:44: "What is sown a natural body rises a spiritual body." He also attached much importance to I Cor. 15:52: "For the trumpet shall sound, and the dead shall rise incorruptible and we shall be changed." Although he does not explicitly relate his doctrine of resurrection to reincarnation, he envisions the resurrection as taking place in a manner quite compatible with reincarnation. Relying heavily on the treatment of resurrection in I Cor. 15:35–58, Origen states: "From the bodies that were sown, men will at the appointed time receive a new body from God endowed according to the merits of each." (*Against Celsus* 5.19.) For Origen, it is unthinkable that the body of flesh and blood should be resurrected into immortality. This body, after all, belongs to the transient world of matter and passes away as all matter must. Origen, the Christian and the Platonist, found it much more likely that a new spiritual body having nothing in common with the material elements of the "natural" body should enjoy the resurrected life. Furthermore, he found ample support for this in Corinthians.

Thus it is perfectly possible for the reincarnationist to assert that the soul passes through many bodies and yet when the time of resurrection comes, it is invested by God with a transformed spiritual body that does not bear the marks and characteristics of any one physical form but is fashioned according to the merits of a man's many lives.

Separation of Body and Soul

The third conflict with reincarnation arising from the Origenist controversy concerns what orthodoxy found to be an unnatural separation of body and soul. There are two aspects to this criticism. First, Origen's critics insisted that the wholeness of man's identity before God consists of both body and soul. They found it objectionable to say, as Origen did, that the soul was essential, while the body was only the incidental vesture of the soul. Second, they devoted much energy to arguing against the preexistence of the soul. They found it contradictory and wrongheaded that the soul should have a disincarnate existence prior to the creation of the body.

The first of these objections—the wholeness of man as body and soul—is already foreshadowed in the controversy over resurrection. Just as the critics took offense at resurrection without a physical body, in like manner they insisted as a general principle that in birth, life, death, and resurrection man is ever a complete creature. Probably the best statement of this is to be found in a letter of the Emperor Justinian to Mennas, patriarch of Constantinople. This letter from the year 543 was the prelude to Origen's condemnation in 553.

Therefore it is clear that souls are not cast into bodies for the punishment of sins as they [the Origenists] foolishly claim, but rather that God fashioned body and soul simultaneously, creating man in his perfected entirety [i.e., body and soul]. (*Letter to Mennas, PG* 86.1, p. 951.)

Plato and Origen had both been of the opinion that the body was inflicted upon the soul to chastise and purify it through the degrading and arduous experiences of incarnate existence. Orthodoxy, however, has chosen to see man as what has been called an "enfleshed soul." Body or soul by itself is but a part of the whole man. Especially significant in this is the Genesis account of man's creation, where, although body and soul are created in tandem, man is not complete until God gave him the breath of life and he became a living soul.

The wholeness of man's nature persists from the time of his creation to his resurrection. Here is Theophilus on the state of resurrected man:

> Once Christ has died, he does not die again. Death loses its power over him. In like manner, our revived bodies do not die second or additional deaths after their resurrection. Neither will death have power over these resurrected bodies of ours, nor will they ever be reduced to nothing, for the coming of Christ has saved man in his entirety [i.e., body and soul]. (Jerome, *Letters* 98.11.)

For Theophilus, God fashioned man in Eden, gave him his blessing, and saw to it that this blessing would follow him, body and soul, to the end. When Christ reconciles man with God, he bestows the privilege of eternal existence upon both body and soul.

Another aspect of the separation of body and soul that concerned Origen's critics was the issue of the preexistence of the soul. Even though preexistence finds support in the New Testament, no feature of Origenism drew more energetic criticism than this. As a general principle the preexistence of the soul would be distasteful to the orthodox, as it allows for disincarnate existence, and Origen's critics managed to put a very fine point on the issue. The Emperor Justinian, for example, frets about the life of disincarnate souls.

> Let the Origenists explain this: If their souls did indeed preexist their bodies, as they claim, in what order of being were they and what were they doing before they entered the body? After all, if they preexisted, they would know where they were and how they got there. But if the Origenists cannot account for themselves—for all this is quite untrue—it is clear that we are dealing with pure nonsense. Or perhaps they may suggest that only after the souls entered the body did they begin to discern and take cognizance of what they were doing. (*Letter to Mennas*, PG 86.1, p. 951.)

Justinian denies here that the disincarnate soul can be sentient and possess self-consciousness. Others—Socrates, Plotinus, and Origen, to name a few—find this perfectly possible. This again raises the question of how one views the human creature. Is he basically a spiritual being, or does he exist only as a composite creature with body and soul? With preexistence goes the assumption that he is essentially spirit.

Indeed the reincarnationist can even find Scriptural support for personal disincarnate preexistence. Origen took Eph. 1:4 as proof for his case: "He chose us in him before the foundation of the world, that we should be holy and without blemish in his sight and love." Jerome, who is just as uncomfortable as Justinian about preexistence, interprets the passage to mean that we preexisted, not in distinct disincarnate form, but simply in the mind of God (*Against Rufinus* 1.22), and from this throng of thoughts God chose the elect before the creation of the world. The distinction is indeed a fine one, for Jerome is asking us to distinguish between that which exists as a soul and that which exists as a thought. What is illuminating for the reincarnationist is that this passage from Ephesians offers very explicit Scriptural testimony for individual preexistence.

Justinian also found numerous difficulties in bringing preexistence into harmony with the Genesis account of man's creation (*Letter to Mennas*, PG 86.1, pp. 953–955). For example, after infusing man's soul into the body and giving him life, God blesses man and sends him off to multiply and exercise dominion over the earth. How can this be reconciled with the Origenist claim that the body is given to chastise the soul? Mennas, using the Genesis account of creation, sees man as a composite of body and soul to whom is given dominion over the earth. Secondly, according to Gen. 2:7, the creation of the body out of clay preceded the infusion of the soul, which surely must contradict the preexistence of the soul.

These objections raise the larger question of how much latitude is to be given in allegorical interpretation of the Scriptures. For the fundamentalist, who cherishes a mental picture of God shaping a mound of clay into human form and then blowing life into it, the proposition of preexistence is indeed questionable. Origen, however, was a very enthusiastic allegorizer and always took pains to find spiritual meaning behind literal meaning. The allegorizer sees Eden as a cosmic event and views the creation of man as something more mysterious and impenetrable than the animation of a ball of dust. If Eden is indeed allegory, as in fact most Christians would now agree, then there are any number of ways to account for the preincarnate life of the soul. For example, one could maintain that the soul infused by God in Eden had preexisted the physical body.

Too Speculative

Origen constructed a theology and a cosmology that account for the rise and fall of creation and the state of man both prior to the beginning and after the end. This was a very natural thing for him to do, for Greek philosophy had always been engaged in inquiry of this sort. It is to be expected of one educated in Greek philosophy, or indeed in any type of speculative thought, to leave no question unconsidered. He does not shy away from certain areas for lack of information. Nor were the Greeks unique in this, for Western education ever since has challenged man to fear no inquiry.

It was in fact in those areas where they lacked specific information that the Greeks were most spectacularly successful, for they relied on speculation. Origen, raised a Christian and keenly devoted to the faith, was also Greek in this regard and possessed to a very high degree that characteristic gift for speculative thought. His first allegiance was always to the faith of the church, but he exercised his imagination to the fullest extent in its service. The result was a complete and consistent theology based upon the Christian Scriptures. A further result was a system that introduced many notions for which the Scriptures provided no evidence. These were not in contradiction to the Scriptures, but simply offered elaboration and speculation where the Scriptures left off. One of the lessons that the fathers of the church had to learn was that speculative thought is of limited use in theology. Man is, to be sure, endowed with intellect and imagination, but these can very easily lead him astray. If a theologian goes too far in speculation, he runs the risk of forcibly imposing his own ideas upon divine revelation. Indeed, he must be doubly cautious, for he writes under the constant vigilance of the church, whose sanction will finally determine whether or not his ideas are acceptable to Christians.

So great are the risks in such an endeavor that Origen would occasionally interrupt his exposition in order to pray for divine guidance. As he ventured into areas where Scripture could not light the way, he came up with a number of conclusions quite compatible with reincarnation. For example, he insists that angels can fall to demonic state and demons can rise to angelic state. Jerome found this very offensive and commented as follows:

From this one may conclude that any rational creature can evolve into any other. This does not just occur suddenly and

once and for all, but goes on continuously. We too will be
angels and demons—demons if we are negligent—and then
the demons will again become angels if they assume virtues.
(Jerome, *Letters* 124.3.)

For Origen, who sees creation as a temporary and finite
manifestation of the Absolute, everything by its very nature
is subject to change and evolution. To the fundamentalist
view, however, there is a menacing fluidity to Origen's con-
ception. The man who reads his Bible literally sees God
creating the world in six days and finding it good on the
seventh. There is a fixity and permanence in things. In the
Genesis account there is a firm finality to God's work that
seems to vouch for the stability of things for all time.

The suggestion that demons could be rising to angels, that
men could be sinking to demons, that the brute-consciousness
of animals could be rising to the self-consciousness of man—
all this seems to threaten the very order of creation. And yet
for the speculative mind such as Origen, creation would be
oppressively rigid and God sadly myopic, were there not this
possibility for dynamic change.

Inherent in the belief in reincarnation is this belief in evolution. The whole purpose of reincarnation is to allow the
soul to grow and perfect itself through the experience gained
in physical form. In fact, for the reincarnationist, as for Origen, God vouches, not for the stability and goodness of creation, but for the perfectability of all he created.

This resistance to speculative thought is implicit in so much
of what is said against Origen. Epiphanius, for example, cannot conceive of a spiritual body coming into man's heavenly
inheritance. Justinian cannot conceive of a soul that preexists
the body. Methodius cannot conceive of man as a disincarnate
creature. All these objections show an unwillingness of the
early church to deal in speculative ideas that do not find
immediate confirmation in the Scriptures.

It is interesting to consider Augustine when faced with

this problem. He had one of the most powerful and naturally speculative minds of the ancient world; yet over and over again he would catch himself, stop short, and look regretfully over the abyss between Scriptural authority and the possibilities suggested by his imagination. Here he is on the very verge of speculation about the origin of the soul:

> I must really confess that, as far as it pertains to the inquiry at hand, I should very much like to know one of the following things: Either I would like to know those things of which I am ignorant as to the origin of the soul, or else I should like to know if it is not for us to learn such things as long as we live here in this world. And yet, what if this is one of those things of which we are told: "Seek not the things that are too high for thee, and search not into the things that are above thy ability: but the things that God hath commanded thee, think of them always and in many of his works be not curious." (Eccl. 3:22.) (Augustine, *On the Soul and Its Origin* 4.4.5.)

Unfortunately the great minds of the church have all too often been called upon to "be not curious." The church fathers of Greco-Roman antiquity found this extremely difficult, for they had been raised in the atmosphere of free inquiry so characteristic of the ancient world.

The Lapse of Memory

The last objection to reincarnation mentioned at the beginning of this chapter is really a technical matter rather than a theological issue. It is worth mentioning only because it is so frequently raised. If reincarnation is indeed true, why do we have no recollection of earlier lives? Justinian raises this question in connection with Luke 16:19–31 (*Letter to Mennas, PG* 86.1, p. 959). The evangelist tells of how Lazarus, the impoverished and sore-ridden beggar, sits at the bosom of Abraham after his passing, while the rich man, whose very crumbs from the table had been a boon to Lazarus, is buried

in hell. The rich man calls out to Abraham in distress, only
to be reminded of the profligate manner of his life. Justinian
takes this as an indication that while man is in the disincarnate
interval after life, he recalls what has transpired during his
incarnate life—after all, the rich man does recall the manner
of his life. If this is so, then surely incarnate man, upon his
return to a new body, should recall the incidents of earlier
incarnations.

Origen does not address himself to this specific problem,
but he may very well have been satisfied with the myth that
Plato used to account for the lapse of recollection between
lives. According to the account of Er at the end of Plato's
Republic (621C), the souls of men drink from the waters
of forgetfulness as they proceed from one life to another.

The Emperor Justinian

Some proponents of reincarnation have suggested that the
edict against Origen was simply the result of a whimsical
quirk of imperial policy. Reincarnation, they affirm, was well
on its way to acceptance within Christendom, when Justinian
stepped in for purely political reasons, employed illegal
methods, and banished it forever. Although there is a glimmer
of truth in this, it is perfectly apparent that ecclesiasts first
took exception to Origen's teachings during his own lifetime
and never ceased to find fault until he was officially anathematized. The reaction against Origen that comes to a head
under Justinian is the accumulation of three hundred years of
reflection on Origenist teachings. The letter of Justinian of
the year 543 owes a clear debt to the work of Origen's critics
over the centuries, and the wording of the fifteen articles of
553 unquestionably represents the position of orthodox Christianity.

What has aroused indignation against Justinian is that his
action against Origen was first prompted by a controversy
between Origenist and anti-Origenist factions in Jerusalem.

It was nothing other than church politics that led to Justinian's edict against Origenism of 543. Furthermore, Justinian flagrantly disregarded the protocol of the church by convening the Council of 553 without the assent of Vigilius, the pope. Technically this means that the anathemas against Origen are not valid and the decree of this council is not binding, for such a council could be convened only by the authority of the pope. It should be pointed out at once, however, that Pope Vigilius accorded his belated approval to the acts of the Council of 553.

Justinian emerges from the Origenist controversy as excessively autocratic, and the council itself stands upon uncertain foundations. Nevertheless, the general sentiment expressed in the tract of 543 and the articles of 553 represent the basic trend of Christianity over the three hundred years following Origen's death.

Conclusion

With the condemnation of Origen, so much that is implied in reincarnation was officially stigmatized as heresy that the possibility of a direct confrontation with this belief was effectively removed from the church. In dismissing Origen from its midst, the church only indirectly addressed itself to the issue of reincarnation. The encounter with Origenism did, however, draw decisive lines in the matter of preexistence, the resurrection of the dead, and the relationship between body and soul. I certainly cannot claim that the contents of this chapter have in any way refuted the reasoning of the church. What an examination of Origen and the church does achieve, however, is to show where the reincarnationist will come into collision with the posture of orthodoxy. The extent to which he may wish to retreat from such a collision is of course a matter of personal conscience.

With the Council of 553 one can just about close the book on this entire controversy within the church. There are merely two footnotes to be added to the story, emerging from church councils in 1274 and 1439. In the Council of Lyons in 1274 it was stated that after death the soul goes *promptly* either to heaven or to hell. On the Day of Judgment all will stand before the tribunal of Christ with their bodies to render account of what they have done. The Council of Florence of 1439 uses almost the same wording to describe the swift passage of the soul either to heaven or to hell. Implicit in both of these councils is the assumption that the soul does not again venture into physical bodies. This assumption, however, is not explicit, and there are in fact aspects of these assertions that might puzzle some of Origen's critics. For example, can one indeed speak of a disincarnate soul sojourning in heaven or hell prior to the time of judgment? Can these postmortem experiences be meaningful to a soul that lacks a body, the supposed instrument of perception and self-consciousness? Any attempt to answer these questions will only give further evidence of what the Origenist controversy has already proven —that these matters fall into the category which Augustine has spoken of as "too high for them and above their ability." Perhaps one of the most essential differences between the reincarnationist and the conventional Christian is that the reincarnationist, like Origen, allows himself more latitude in determining what is too high and above his ability.

V

REINCARNATION
AND THE NEW TESTAMENT

One of the essential features of Christianity is its uncompromising respect for Scriptural authority. Although the doctrines and beliefs of individual ecclesiasts and denominations are various and changeable, the Scriptures provide the firm rock upon which these many creeds stand. Hence it must be asked: Does reincarnation find support in the Christian Scriptures? Although this question eludes a conclusive and final answer, there are to be found in the New Testament a number of passages compatible with reincarnation. Moreover, a plausible case can be made that Jesus himself was acquainted with reincarnation.

Before examining the Scriptures, however, the serious Christian should ask himself: What difference would it make if twentieth-century scholars could offer conclusive proof that reincarnation was taught in the early church? Christian doctrine, after all, is what the faithful accept at any given time, and it has been generally assumed that the Holy Spirit is guiding and inspiring Christendom in its faith throughout the ages. Those who wish to expand, alter, or reshape Christianity by uncovering so-called "lost teachings" of the early church should not minimize the fact that men of great intelligence and piety have prayed earnestly for help in the formulation of Christian doctrine. Anyone who proposes a new and revolutionary change of direction should recognize both the validity and, indeed, the sanctity of the past. After surviving persecutions, heresies, and wars for almost two thousand years, Christianity has shown a miraculous ability to define and maintain its own unique character in a cultural setting where compromise and misinterpretation are rife.

No matter how the creed of Christians may change in the future, this in no way lessens or tarnishes the rightness of the past. For example, the doctrine of election—the belief that only a small and select number will be saved from eternal damnation—was a great inspiration to Christians during the persecutions under the Roman emperors. Now, however, that we live in a truly ecumenical world and are not so earnest about election, we are inclined to take this metaphorically rather than forever exclude anyone from the love of God. Thus as Christianity becomes a more universal religion, the meaning of the Scriptures shifts accordingly.

Just as changing times have caused Christians to alter their attitude about the doctrine of election, so also attitudes about the soul and afterlife are changing under the impact of new philosophies winning popularity in the West. My purpose in this chapter is to accommodate as responsibly as possible the words of the New Testament to these changing attitudes. Such proof as can be given for reincarnation in the New Testament is offered merely as an open door to those who feel that their spiritual life would be enriched by the doctrine of reincarnation. Perhaps some will find satisfaction in discovering that reincarnation can be advanced on the testimony of Christian Scriptures.

A few words should be said in advance about how one approaches the New Testament. Those who interpret the Scriptures without heed of context or setting usually fall into two categories. Either they are zealots so passionate in defense of their theory that they disregard the very useful findings of generations of scholars, or else they possess a spiritual authority that places their interpretations beyond the reach of critical scholarship.

Of the first category nothing more need be said, save that they have done much to trivialize and undermine the case for reincarnation in the eyes of thoughtful Christians.

The second category, those with spiritual authority, is much more difficult to come to grips with. There is a tradition, even within orthodox Christianity, of unveiling the mystical or spiritual meaning that lies hidden beneath the surface of the Scriptures. This, of course, immediately raises the question of determining whose spiritual meaning is the correct one. Within the Catholic Church the problem has been somewhat simplified by the canonization of thinkers such as Augustine and Thomas Aquinas. It is assumed that their interpretations were inspired by the Holy Spirit and hence are binding for all Catholics. There are others, however, who lack such official recognition and yet, independently of the church, they possess charismatic authority, at least for their followers. For such interpreters, the evangelist or apostle is addressing himself on the surface to those literalists who rely upon their reason and the commonly accepted meanings of words. Below the surface, however, lies a wholly different meaning accessible to those gifted with intuition.

There is no rational test for the validity of such intuitions beyond their capacity to win acceptance and enrich men's spiritual lives. An excellent example of this sort is the statement of Joseph Smith, the prophet and founder of Mormonism, that when Jesus claims to have "other sheep that are not of this fold" (John 10:16) he means the Mormons living at the time of his ministry on the North American continent. Although there is not a hint of Mormons or North America to be found in the background of the New Testament, the charismatic authority of Joseph Smith is such that millions of Mormons have accepted this interpretation and derived spiritual comfort in knowing that Christ thought of them, even while he walked the earth. Who is to say that this is false?

There are such charismatic figures who have proclaimed reincarnation in the New Testament on the basis of their inspired interpretations. These men have been believed by their adherents, and for many they have imparted a new life to the Christian Scriptures. Most traditional Christians, how-

ever, insist upon a reasoned argument based upon known
sources, and it is chiefly to them that I am speaking.

Jesus and John the Baptist
as Believers in Reincarnation

On the basis of contemporary Biblical scholarship a plausible case can be made that Jesus and John the Baptist accepted reincarnation, having learned of it through the Essenes.
Living at the time of Christ, the Essenes were a Jewish sect
that had fled the corruption and congestion of the city in
favor of a simple and austere life of prayer and farming in
the desert. They are known to us from antiquity chiefly
through the Jewish historian Josephus, although they are also
mentioned much more briefly by Philo, Pliny the Elder, and
some of the church fathers. More recently they have been in
the news through the discovery of the Dead Sea Scrolls.

We know that they lived very pure lives subject to a strict
regimen of prayer, baptism, communal sacred meals, and
work in the fields. Not only did they inhabit their barren
desert retreats, such as the one at Qumran where the scrolls
were found, but they also had traveling members and repre-
sentatives throughout the cities of Judea.

Whether or not they specifically believed in reincarnation
cannot be claimed as a certainty. In one passage (*Antiquities
of the Jews* 15.371), Josephus states that they lived by a
Pythagorean regimen. As we know, Pythagoras was *the* name
associated in antiquity with the doctrine of reincarnation.
Scholars have made much of this statement in Josephus and
have found many points of similarity between the Pythagorean religious orders and those of the Essenes. The following points have been especially emphasized: ritual bathing,
no swearing of oaths, continence, sanctity through asceticism,
pure food and clothing, prayers to the sun at the beginning
and end of the day, and the belief in a divine, immortal soul
for man.

The similarities are so striking and so numerous that the

Essene order may very well be the direct outgrowth of contact between Pythagoreanism and Jewish culture. Whatever their origin, however, there are a sufficient number of non-Jewish elements in Essene beliefs and practices to encourage the supposition that the Essenes came in contact with alien cultures. For example, in the Scrolls, life is frequently viewed as a dualistic struggle between darkness and light—a wholly non-Jewish idea that may have come in under the influence of the Mazdean religion of Persia. Furthermore, by regarding the soul as divine, the Essenes moved entirely out of the assumptions of conventional Judaism.

Whether or not they believed specifically in cycles of rebirth cannot be proven. Josephus, in speaking of the Essene doctrine of the soul, uses language very reminiscent of both Pythagoras and Plato. He speaks of the soul as immortal and indestructible and as being momentarily imprisoned in the body (*Jewish War* 2.154). Once the soul is rid of the chains of flesh and is set free from the bondage of earthly life, it goes on either to the Isles of the Blessed for reward or to Hades for punishment (*ibid.*, 2.156).

Although Josephus does not specify whether souls come back for additional births, he does assign preexistence and divinity to them—two essential features of reincarnation. His use of the Isles of the Blessed and of Hades almost certainly connects him with the Pythagoreans, who in turn appropriated this notion from Homer (*Odyssey* 4.562 ff.) and then imposed their own theology of the timeless, deathless soul sojourning in the fetters of the body. Implicit in such a view is the assumption that souls will undergo several incarnations, for they do not achieve perfection within a single life. Most likely the vision of the afterlife implied by Josephus is the same as the one stated by Plato at the end of the *Republic* (614)—namely, that souls proceed to Hades or the Isles of the Blessed in accordance with merits. Once they have either enjoyed the benefits or reaped the punishment that accrued during earthly life, they return once again to physical bodies. Such, at least, would be the logical conclusion, inasmuch as

Josephus states that the Essenes viewed the afterlife in the same way as the "sons of the Greeks" (*Jewish War* 2.155).

Assuming that the Essenes believed in reincarnation, is it possible to establish any connection between Jesus of Nazareth and this sect? As to Jesus himself having been an Essene, the prevailing opinion of Biblical scholars is that he was not. In the teaching of Jesus there is nothing of the asceticism, legalism, and secrecy characteristic of the Essenes. On the other hand, the messianic expectations of the Essenes are often similar to those filled by Jesus, for they lived in constant hope of a new order of things that would be ushered in by a savior. Indeed, there is much in Essenism that can be referred to as a "foretaste of Christianity," to use the phrase of Ernest Renan, the famous nineteenth-century biographer of Jesus.

If there was any contact between Essenism and the life of Christ, the most likely intermediary was John the Baptist. There are features both of the life and the teaching of John the Baptist that strongly suggest association with the Essenes. According to Luke 1:80, for example, John passed the period of his life prior to his ministry out in the desert. He preached a very harsh gospel of penitence, chastising the crowds that came to him with words such as: "Brood of vipers! who has shown you how to flee the wrath to come?" (Luke 3:7.) John was also most insistent about the cleansing waters of baptism, a point of similarity with the Essenes that has become even more evident since the discovery of the Dead Sea Scrolls. Lastly, John's role as the forerunner of a savior who shall usher in a new age is very reminiscent of the Essene messiah, who was also preceded by a forerunner. When we consider these three points of similarity, we have a composite picture that points very persuasively to Essene background.

In establishing the link between Jesus and Essenism, it remains only to determine the connection between Jesus and John the Baptist. This presents no serious difficulty, as Jesus clearly came under the influence of John the Baptist in preparing for his ministry. Not only did he receive baptism from

John, but at one point he even states explicitly that he was the disciple of John (Matt. 11:11). This is a passage generally mistranslated as: "Yet he who is least in the kingdom of heaven is greater than he."

Scholars have called into question this translation and the resulting interpretation, for the traditional translation depends upon rendering the Greek word for "less" or "smaller" as "least." More defensible is: "He who is less [Jesus, the disciple] is greater than he [John the Baptist] in the kingdom of heaven." Seen in this light, the passage would be a claim on the part of Jesus that although he had at one time been less than John in the here and now, he is greater in the Kingdom of Heaven. The tradition for such an interpretation is of great antiquity and also has the endorsement of some of the leading Biblical scholars of this century. Among the fathers of the church, Jerome, Origen, Hilary, and Chrysostom all interpreted this passage to mean that although John had once been greater than Jesus here on earth, the situation was reversed in the Kingdom of Heaven. It has more recently been pointed out that the word "younger" or "lesser" is in fact the rabbinic term for a disciple. A further problem with the more conventional translation ("Yet he who is least in the kingdom of heaven is greater than he [John]") is that with these words Jesus is explicitly excluding John from the Kingdom of Heaven.

For one who wishes to establish a direct connection between Jesus and the doctrine of reincarnation, here is a defensible argument based upon the working assumptions of recent New Testament scholarship. The most serious problem in this line of argument arises from the contradictions between Josephus and the Dead Sea Scrolls. The Scrolls envision a brief and tenuous life for the soul, thus raising the question whether the Essenes either had various beliefs about the soul or whether in fact the people of Qumran described in the Scrolls may be wholly different from the Essenes of Josephus. Whatever the answer to this problem, the testimony of

Josephus, a first-century Jew, is not to be taken lightly, and on his authority the Essenes seem to be believers in reincarnation.

Did Jesus Actually Preach Reincarnation?

To determine with any confidence whether or not Jesus actually preached reincarnation requires an awareness of when the Scriptures are recording his own words, as contrasted to when the Evangelist is assigning to Jesus a probable or appropriate utterance. In their efforts to sort out the words of Jesus from those of the Evangelists, scholars have endeavored to discover the beliefs that would have been peculiar to the Evangelists but may not date back to the time of Jesus. From what we can gather of the background and experience of the Evangelists, it is wholly improbable that any of them accepted reincarnation. Hence, if there is any overt or explicit endorsement of reincarnation, it would have had to slip in through inadvertence.

Jesus had been crucified about thirty years before the first Gospel was written and, although a generation of Christians had been embellishing and interpreting his words, there can be no question that much of the Gospel narrative is his authentic utterance. If one can identify the sayings of Jesus that seem to go against the Christianity of A.D. 60 or 70, then we are quite possibly dealing with his own words. If, for example, there were overt references to reincarnation in the Gospels, these almost certainly could not derive from the Evangelists, but might well belong to an earlier tradition, deriving even from Jesus himself. Christ may have said things that suggest or even clearly point to reincarnation, and the Gospel writers, although personally opposed to this belief, may have recorded these words without realizing fully what they imply.

The Man Blind from Birth

The question can now be asked: Do the Scriptures provide any such overt references to reincarnation on the part of

Jesus? There is one episode in particular from the healing miracles of Christ that seems to point to reincarnation: "And as he was passing by, he saw a man blind from birth. And his disciples asked him, 'Rabbi, who has sinned, this man or his parents, that he should be born blind?' Jesus answered, 'Neither has this man sinned, nor his parents, but the works of God were to be made manifest in him.'" (John 9:1 ff.) Jesus then goes on to prepare a salve that results in the restoration of sight.

In interpreting this episode, commentators have pointed out that the example of the man blind from birth is occasionally used to illustrate the problem of divine justice. How can we grasp the justice of an all-loving God, if he will allow a man to enter into the world with such a crushing handicap? Such afflictions, of which Job is perhaps the classic example, show that apparently unwarranted suffering is in fact the prelude to bountiful blessings. The story of the blind man also conveys a message very common to John's Gospel, namely, that Jesus dispels man's darkness.

The answer that Jesus gives to the question of the disciples shows that he is much more interested in "making manifest the works of God" than he is in the origins or cause of the man's blindness. Nevertheless, there is a glaring inconsistency in the question posed by the disciples. They ask the Lord if the man himself could have committed the sin that led to his blindness. Given the fact that the man has been blind from birth, we are confronted with a provocative question. When could he have made such transgressions as to make him blind at birth? The only conceivable answer is in some prenatal state. The question as posed by the disciples explicitly presupposes prenatal existence. It will also be noted that Christ says nothing to dispel or correct the presupposition. Here is incontrovertible support for a doctrine of human preexistence.

The fact that Jesus says nothing against preexistence here provides a fine example of how an alien doctrine might escape the vigilance of the Evangelist and slip into the Scriptures. It is perfectly reasonable to surmise on the basis of this episode that Jesus and his followers accepted preexistence and thought so little of it that the question of prenatal sin did not even call for an answer.

That reincarnation is implicit here has escaped the notice of most commentators. It is interesting to note, however, that in his *Commentary on John*, Rudolf Bultmann, probably the most distinguished New Testament scholar of this century, recognizes the reincarnationist undercurrent here and repudiates any Buddhist influence. Such a reaction is, of course, perfectly proper, as there is no known way for Buddhism to have penetrated to Jesus and his disciples. To write off Buddhism, however, does not remove the fact that we have here an explicit statement of prenatal existence with all its implications for *karma* and reincarnation.

There is probably no more persuasive passage in the New Testament than this one to support the case that Jesus and his followers accepted or at least were aware of reincarnation.

John the Baptist and Elijah

Also very suggestive of reincarnation is the episode where Jesus identifies John the Baptist as Elijah.

"For all the prophets and the law have prophesied until John. And if you are willing to receive it, he is Elias who was to come." (Matt. 11:13–14.)

"And the disciples asked him, saying, 'Why then do the scribes say that Elias must come first?' But he answered them and said, 'Elias indeed is to come and will restore all things. But I say to you that Elias has come already, and they did not know him, but did to him whatever they wished. So also shall the Son of Man suffer at their hand.' Then the disciples understood that he had spoken of John the Baptist." (Matt. 17:10–13.)

Here again is a clear statement of preexistence. Despite the edict of the Emperor Justinian and the counter reaction to Origen, there is firm and explicit testimony for preexistence in both the Old and the New Testament. Indeed, the ban against Origen notwithstanding, contemporary Christian scholarship acknowledges preexistence as one of the elements of Judeo-Christian theology.

As for the John the Baptist–Elijah episode, there can be little question as to its purpose. By identifying the Baptist as Elijah, Jesus is identifying himself as the Messiah. Throughout the Gospel narrative there are explicit references to the signs that will precede the Messiah. Thus in Mark 1:2, in Matt. 11:10, and in Luke 7:27 there is a direct reminiscence of the prophetic statement in Mal. 3:1: "Behold I send my angel, and he shall prepare the way before my face. And presently the Lord, whom you desire, shall come to his temple. Behold he cometh, saith the Lord of Hosts." The same prophecy is reinforced in Mal. 4:5: "Behold I will send you Elias the prophet, before the coming of the great and dreadful day of the Lord." This is one of the many messianic promises of the Old Testament. One of the signs that the true messiah has come, according to this passage from Malachi, is that he be preceded by a forerunner, by an Elijah.

Both Elijah and John the Baptist are manifestations of a preexistent type: the forerunner. The meaning of preexistence here is that which possesses eternal disincarnate existence combined with at least the latent faculty to manifest on the physical plane. That preexistence implies reincarnation was perfectly obvious to the critics of Origen. If that which has eternal, disincarnate existence is capable of one manifestation or incarnation, then why not several? With the ban against Origen in 553, however, Christians have simply ceased to give serious thought to the possibility of reincarnation. Preexistence has been written off along with its corollary of reincarnation, and yet here we are confronted once again with preexistence. Before the anathemas against Origen, Bible commentators were quite aware that the Elijah–John equation suggests reincarnation. In his commentary on Matthew, Jerome argues against reincarnation (PL 26, p. 74), insisting on the interpretation that arises from Luke 1:17—that John came not in the person of Elijah but in his "spirit and power."

What is important about Christ's words, however, is that they are unequivocal. In order to make his identity as the Messiah known to his followers, Christ vouches for the absolute identity between Elijah and John the Baptist. Anything less than absolute identity undermines Christ's claims to messiahship. As the disciples are able to accept John the Baptist as Elijah, to that extent they are able to grasp Christ as the Messiah. For the messianic prophecy of Malachi to be fully realized, John the Baptist must *be* Elijah. If one accepts the messianic forerunner as a preexistent type of whom Elijah and John are both incarnations, then it is clear that John comes not just "in the spirit and power" of Elijah but in his person as well—the direct, palpable, incarnate reappearance of Elijah.

The Preexistent Christ

The most conspicuous instance of preexistence in the New Testament is Christ himself. This is made perfectly apparent in Phil. 2:6–8: ". . . who [Christ], though he was by nature God, did not consider being God a thing to be clung to, but emptied himself, taking the nature of a slave and being made like unto men. And appearing in the form of a man, he humbled himself, becoming obedient to death, even to death on a cross." Here Paul is saying that Christ first divested himself of his divine majesty before embarking upon his earthly ministry. The opening words of John's Gospel affirm the same principle: "In the beginning was the Word, and the Word was with God." (John 1:1.) This line of thought culminates in v. 14: "And the Word was made flesh, and dwelt among us." Not only do we have these statements from Paul and John, but Christ himself asserts his own preexistence: "Before Abraham came to be, I am." (John 8:58.)

Implicit in all these statements is the recognition that the majesty and greatness of Christ are of such an order as to precede and outlast secular time. It is perfectly apparent that

Christ exists eternally and indestructibly. Nor does his existence in any way depend upon the presence of a body.

The preexistence of Christ does not, of course, guarantee the preexistence of the human soul. However, to the extent that Christ presents himself as an attainable example to mankind, human preexistence is not to be dismissed. In a passage such as John 14:12, Christ seems very willing to rank his followers as even more than his equal: "He who believes in me, the works that I do he also shall do and greater than these shall he do." If Christ is an example for man in his works, then why not in his stature as well?

Conclusion

Any attempt to argue the case for or against reincarnation in the New Testament is seriously hampered by the fact that the New Testament concerns itself very little with the prenatal and postmortem life of man. The basic concern is with the Kingdom proclaimed by Christ and the way in which men accept it in the here and now. If the case that I have made here for reincarnation seems either far-fetched or overly ingenious, I can only say that it is at least as good as the counter case to be made on the basis of Scripture.

If the church had accepted reincarnation, the two passages I have dealt with would certainly have been crucial. Had reincarnation then become an unquestioned premise of Christendom, one could enlist many other passages in support of it, such as Eph. 1:4 and Rev. 3:12. As it is, however, Christian doctrine, and with it the trend of Biblical scholarship, has gone against reincarnation. Thus anyone wishing to argue the case for reincarnation is handicapped, for modern research has occupied itself with questions that shed very little light on this subject. Nevertheless, the convinced reincarnationist may perhaps be encouraged to find that an intriguing case can be made on the basis of existing materials and research.

VI

REINCARNATION
AND CHRISTIAN LIFE

The natural conclusion to this book is to suggest a pattern of Christian life compatible with the belief of reincarnation. Since, however, many aspects of such a pattern have already been dealt with in the previous chapters, it remains now to touch on a few features of Christian life not yet discussed. What I hope will emerge is a general overview of Christian life consistent both with itself and with the belief in reincarnation.

Any pattern or system of spiritual life is no more than a synthetic creation put together of disparate ideas, and it possesses institutional authority for the Christian only when ratified by church council. Personal and charismatic authority, however, comes when an individual gives assent to a system as descriptive of his own beliefs. One discovers, moreover, that the articles of faith of ardent and faithful believers vary greatly—which only gives further evidence that creeds derive their authority not so much from institutional approval as from the significance with which the individual invests them.

The preliminary to any Christian creed is a life in Jesus Christ subject to the will of the Father. Such a statement entails two things: first, that the individual accord to Jesus Christ the supreme position in his life, and second, that he try to subordinate every desire and impulse to the will of God. These are two fixed points in relation to which he may proceed to plot the course of his spiritual life. Whatever theological embellishments he adds will be based upon Scripture, the teaching of the church, and his own intuition, and, depending upon the individual and his denomination, he will give greater authority to the first, second, or third of these factors.

The Christian who wishes to assimilate reincarnation into his beliefs will clearly give more authority to intuition than to anything else. It should be evident from the preceding chapters, however, that he is not completely without support from Scripture and that, although the teaching of the church is against him, the picture that emerges from the history of dogma is not entirely clear-cut.

The basic posture of the Christian reincarnationist as well as the opposing arguments of orthodoxy emerge from the Origenist controversy discussed in Chapter IV. Once man is viewed as the divine and eternal spark of God, the entire trajectory of the religious life is determined: man is infallibly moving toward full, conscious realization of his own divinity. As we have seen, such a view entails a decided shift of emphasis in the religious life for the conventional Christian. In addition to the topics covered in Chapter IV—the saving grace of Christ, the resurrection of the body, the preexistence of the soul, and the distinction between body and soul—the following topics deserve brief mention: evolution, the role of faith, the end of time, otherworldliness, activism, knowledge of God, and Christ as Savior.

Evolution

One of the most essential features of the reincarnationist view is evolution, ensuring that every soul comes to perfection before God. The journey may be arduous and protracted, but the cycles of birth and death have the implicit guarantee of final success. It is evident from the Origenist controversy that traditional Christianity has resisted the concept of evolution. Origen himself saw evolution as an irresistible tide that would finally carry all things to perfection. The critics of Origen were troubled, however, by the suggestion that Satan himself should finally be restored to God's favor. They preferred to see a more stable fixity in the world as God constituted it and to insist that certain things remain essentially and inalienably fallen. Just as God chose the elect before the beginning of the world, so also he has set apart certain things for eternal separation from himself.

An instance of this type of thinking is to be found in Augustine's *City of God*. In the persons of Cain and Abel, Augustine sees a prototype of self-love set against love for God, and this division runs as a fissure through all creation, separating what will be saved from what will be damned. There is an absolute, set fixity to things, which will require a final parting of ways. Some people, known to God from the beginning of time, will be reconciled to him; others, equally well identified in the divine providence, will not be so fortunate.

If one accepts such a line of demarcation, the dimensions of evolution are sorely limited. Everything stands on one side of the line or the other, and God's work in the world is not so much progressive and evolutionary as it is a matter of separating the wheat from the chaff. In such a system the restoration of all creation is frustrated and stultified. The implications of this have troubled many theologians. How can God, the very essence of love, bring creatures into being, only to cast some of them from himself forever? Here is a paradox out of which reincarnation and the concept of spiritual evolution can lead the way.

In fact, to embrace the doctrine of reincarnation is to accept the necessity of evolution. Reincarnation makes sense both ethically and theologically in that it demands and ensures the evolution of all. Much more promising and hopeful than Augustine's view of Cain and Abel prefiguring the division between the saved and the damned is the treatment of Esau and Jacob by Origen. Jacob merely had greater merit from earlier lives, but the ultimate salvation of Cain is no less certain than that of Esau. (*On First Principles* 9.7.)

Theologians as ancient as Origen and as recent as Teilhard de Chardin have run afoul of orthodoxy by all but eliminating damnation and allowing God to reclaim all things. Such a philosophy stands upon a positive and optimistic view of life that simply rebels at the thought that God would reject anything he had made. Such optimism finds ample support in Scripture, and it comes as no surprise that a favorite passage of both Origen and Teilhard was the assurance of the apostle that someday God will be "all in all" (I Cor. 15:28). For those Christians who see God's love as all-embracing, a doctrine of comprehensive evolution and restoration is especially attractive.

The Role of Faith

For the reincarnationist, faith takes on a significance somewhat different from what it has for the traditional Christian. Probably the classic definition of faith within Christianity is to be found in Heb. 11:1: "Now faith is the substance of things hoped for, the evidence of things not seen." What is essential in this definition is that it calls for a total investment and commitment to something that is only partially disclosed. The most spectacular examples of faith of this kind are to be found in the martyrs of the church—people who went confidently and serenely to their death in the hope that they would inherit another kingdom far above the tribulations of this world. This is total investment on the basis of partial disclosure. That such faith is an inspiring and moving spectacle is eloquently attested by the fathers of the early church, many of whom were originally converted to Christianity by the faith and courage of the martyrs.

This type of Christian faith works at closing the gap between the here and now and the final consummation of God's plan for man. Such faith requires great psychic energy, for the consummation is remote—it lies at the end of time—and the rewards of faith are only dimly perceived in the here and now.

If, however, one accepts the premises of reincarnation, faith is no longer called upon to build a bridge across the span of the ages from finitude to the infinite. The infinite is already fully present right in the here and now. Those who have achieved mystic union, the goal of contemplation, all claim to have made that leap from the finite to the infinite. God's Kingdom is no farther away than the innermost kernel of one's own consciousness. If we take each man in his essence to be Atman, a divine spark, then man no longer needs to reach across the ages to see God face to face.

Seen in this light, the concept of faith is altered considerably. One of the great difficulties for the traditional Christian is to make his hopeful and tentative outreach across the chasm of time. Often he is inclined to be fainthearted, either because the evidence for the goal is tenuous or because the chasm is so large. To live his religion truly and deeply, the traditional Christian must carry a heavy load upon his faith. This weight is radically shifted for the reincarnationist. His faith is focused on the much more immediate and palpable goal of discovering that God is within. In this case, faith is the growing conviction that comes as the intimations of God's presence become more powerful. It is not so much a long-term investment in "things hoped for" or "things not seen" as the direct and experiential knowledge that arises out of glimpsing one's own divinity.

In saying this, I have no intention of demeaning traditional Christian faith. It is a force which helped to transform the Roman Empire from paganism to Christianity, and it has provided examples that have uplifted and changed the lives of many men. In fact, the long-term faith of expectation and the immediate faith of experience are by no means mutually exclusive. Every spiritual aspirant enjoys moments when his faith receives palpable assurance, and likewise all are called upon to stake the very real present upon the uncertain future.

The End of Time

One of the major ingredients feeding into the background of the New Testament is apocalyptic Judaism. The history of the Jewish people has been one of almost uninterrupted hardship, and as a result they have often looked yearningly toward the day when God will reveal his justice, punish the persecutors, and bring secular time to an end. Christianity has inherited this legacy, and even now there are Christian sects that expect the end momentarily.

At the time of the apocalypse there will be a winnowing, and those with merit will see God no longer "through a glass darkly," while those who have fallen short will be sent to their appropriate punishment. This view differs in two ways from that of the reincarnationist. First, the reincarnationist is not especially interested in the end of the world, for he realizes that until he has progressed to the point of God-realization, the Lord will continue to provide a stage for the drama of life. Secondly, he believes that he need not wait until the end of time to see God as he really is. For every man there awaits a personal apocalypse as soon as he has realized God.

Such a view is especially suitable to the present age. Christians are no longer persecuted for their beliefs and only a very few denominations speak with any enthusiam about the end of the world. Generally speaking, Christianity has gained for itself a secure and lasting place, and Christians are of the opinion that the world is going to be around for a long time to come. It is perhaps reassuring to reflect that God's self-disclosure is available to every man right now, rather than at the unconceivably remote end of galactic time.

Otherworldliness and Activism

Christians who have been raised with the values of the West may see in reincarnation a quietistic and otherworldly flight from the realities of this world. What the reincarnationist seems to be saying is that the Atman, the true Self, is the only reality, and all else is merely a dreamlike deception. If this be the case, then one may well ask if there is any need for brotherly love and the good works that make this world a better place for all of us. We look to India, where Hinduism, far from transforming this world for the better, seems to have helped to create a level of suffering and privation without equal.

To the charge of quietism I would answer with this passage from the *Gita*:

Not even for a moment can anyone remain free of action. Whether he wills it or not, every man is created to action by the very structure of the world. (*Bhagavad-Gita* 3.5.)

The Westerner who turns to the doctrine of reincarnation is in no way required to adopt the passivity of the East. Implicit in the religious life is great dynamism. He who embarks upon the spiritual life has undertaken the most ambitious venture that man can make: to pass from the finitude of his own life to the infinity of God. This cannot succeed without energetic involvement.

For the reincarnationist, this energy proceeds along two paths. One of them goes within. By turning the full force of his attention inward, he cultivates the presence of God himself. Plain common sense shows, however, that a life spent solely in contemplation is not even half a life. Whether one's beliefs are Eastern or Western, the tumultuous activity of nature testifies to God's own dynamic activity. One of the most forceful reminders of God's activity is the power of love that draws men together, sustains civilization, and purges the taint of selfishness from human character.

The spiritual life is often spoken of as a razor's edge, a very apt metaphor for one who would discover the proper balance between activity and contemplation, the welfare of humanity

and the welfare of his own soul. We are just as much offended
by the man who turns his back on humanity in order to know
God as we are by the self-righteous do-gooder, constantly
thrusting his uncalled-for "help" upon others while heedless of
the beam in his own eye.

According to those who have achieved it, the joy of God-
realization is enhanced to the extent that one is able to show
the way to others. Thus, although every man comes to the
spiritual path as an individual and advances along it in soli-
tude, he will find his life immeasurably enriched when he
makes common cause with his fellowman.

Knowledge of God

In a famous and frequently misquoted statement, the
church father Tertullian says the death of God's Son is be-
lievable because it is preposterous and his resurrection is a
certainty because it is impossible (*On the Flesh of Christ* 5).
These paradoxical words offer a deep insight into the very
essence of Christianty. Christians have traditionally assumed
that what little they can know of God while still confined to
their mortal body is "seen as through a glass darkly." The profound and mysterious plan according to which God has dis-
posed things can only confound the feeble and presumptuous
intellect of man. Tertullian discovered strength and assurance
in reflecting upon the absurdity at the core of the Christian
creed—that God's Son could actually die and then, having
died, could be raised three days later. To accept such a proposition fully and unreservedly is to admit that the powers of
reason and logic are inadequate to deal with the ways of God.

Inherent in traditional Christianity is the belief that certain
things should be relegated to the category of mystery. Indeed,
it is a logical necessity that man as the creature of God should
be unable to grasp fully his Creator's ways. The problem
that such limitations create was very vividly illustrated by
the fate of Origen. As a Hellene and a philosopher, he craved

answers and finality from the Absolute. This eventually led him into heresy, for he was most reluctant to accept paradox and mystery where he thought reason could lead the way.

In this matter the reincarnationist is very much on the side of Origen. If man is a divine essence and is progressing toward a point of perfect union with God, then there can be nothing of God that will remain obscure. Since God is the measure of man, all his ways must be knowable. Furthermore, if man is indeed a spark of God, it makes no sense that man should appease and frustrate his God-given curiosity with mysteries and paradoxes. Those who have come to the final point of divine union assure us that in that moment all mystery falls away. Unfortunately the maddening paradox remains that words fail to convey that which finally stands revealed at the pinnacle of union.

What is important is the attitude of one who believes that man is divine. Rather than submit to being enshrouded in a "cloud of unknowing," he is fully confident of unraveling the ultimate questions. Herein I believe the reincarnationist has a very real boon: Taking union with the Absolute as his spiritual goal, he is willing to step up boldly to questions of final significance, assured that they will someday disclose their secret to him.

The Role of Christ

As was evident in the Origenist controversy, traditional Christianity has taken exception to any system that would seem to minimize the redemptive role of Christ. Origen's critics indignantly asked: What need was there of Christ's mission if man is to incarnate again and again until he comes to realize the purity of the very Godhead? If all men are inalienable sons of God, what need is there of a Christ to ensure their adoption into God's Kingdom?

It is indeed true that he who is already a particle of God does not need redemption in the strict sense of the word. To redeem in its original sense is to buy back or make good. Thus in traditional Christianity Christ is seen as the One who, with his own blood, buys back for man that state of grace which was forfeited in the Garden of Eden. Man, unworthy and unable to achieve his own perfection, must have a mediator who by proxy can make good his original defection from God.

If, as the reincarnationist believes, man himself must make his peace with God, what place is given to Christ? Nothing really changes, except that vicarious atonement is done away with. The person and ministry of Christ is in no way altered. He came into the world as the Son of God in order to inspire man with a tangible manifestation of God's love. Spiritual life grows in both power and sweetness as one is able to cultivate and feel the living presence of Christ. He is, however, no longer the savior who delivers from damnation, but rather is the one who provides through his life and unfailing help vivid assurances of God's love.

The message of Christ's ministry and his suffering on the cross are in no way minimized for the reincarnationist. In the person of Christ he sees the direct emissary of God, sent because "God so loved the world." The cross is not so much an act of atonement for man's sin as the price Christ was willing to pay in order to assure men of God's love. Salvation takes place then, not as redemption from the fall, but rather as the hope and confidence that every man stands to gain by claiming Christ's love as his own. To be saved by Christ means to know that one stands in the unfailing light of God's love.

Conclusion

Does it make any ultimate difference in the religious life whether or not one believes in reincarnation? This question brings us back to the considerations raised in the introduction. If doctrine and beliefs are merely the by-product of the unique and primal encounter with God, then it matters very little what one believes. I have been using as a minimal definition of Christianity: "A life in Jesus Christ subject to the will of the Father." Such a life makes no specific demands in terms of doctrine or creed.

Even now as I look back on the research and thought I have devoted to a defense of reincarnation in this book, I find that there are much greater priorities in the religious life than whether one does or does not accept a particular theological tenet. Those who are still irresolute on the question of reincarnation, or indeed those who are emphatically resolute in one direction or another, possess no special advantage before God. The only possible advantage that the reincarnationist may claim over those who are unresolved or opposed is that he has a reasonable and consistent theory to account for the prenatal and postmortem life of the soul as well as an explanation for the apparent absurdities in the dispensation of divine justice. The peace and joy that arise from the spiritual life, however, depend in no way upon the particular creed one confesses.

A GUIDE
TO PRIMARY SOURCES

By omitting footnotes and secondary sources, I do not wish to conceal the fact that I have benefited enormously from the works of scholars in the fields of ancient philosophy, church history, New Testament, and Hinduism. Since, however, this book is not directed primarily to other scholars, I have chosen not to draw attention to the very considerable secondary material I have consulted. The following paragraphs are intended to provide the general reader with a brief assessment of the most important primary sources employed in writing this book.

HINDUISM

The concept of reincarnation pervades Hinduism just as that of fall and redemption pervades Christianity. Hence the following entries offer no more than a few classic statements on the subject of rebirth.

Upanishads. The earliest formulation of *samsara*, or rebirth, is found in the *Upanishads*. The following are representative passages: *Brihadaranyaka Up.* 4.4.3–5; 6.2.1–2; *Chandogya Up.* 5.10.7; *Katha Up.* 2.2.6–7; *Mundaka Up.* 3.2.1–3.

Bhagavad-Gita. The principal teaching concerning the eternal nature of the soul is found in chapter 2, verses 16–30. Probably the most widely known statement on rebirth from Hindu scriptures is 2.22.

GRECO-ROMAN ANTIQUITY

Reincarnation found its way into Greek philosophy through Orphism and Pythagoreanism. Both of these sects lack primary documents, and our knowledge of them comes from later sources. The most detailed and subtle discussion of reincarnation in classical thought is found in the works of Plato. Although he touches on the subject frequently, the fullest accounts are to be found in the *Republic* 614–621, the *Phaedrus* 245–252, and the *Phaedo* 73–77.

Early Christianity was influenced by Platonism through the intermediary of Neoplatonism, whose principal spokesman is Plotinus. A convenient abridgment of his works is available in the Signet Edition (1964), *The Essential Plotinus,* tr. by Elmer O'Brien. The standard full-length English version of his works is that of Stephen MacKenna, published by Pantheon Books (1957).

THE ESSENES

When using the Essenes as a source on reincarnation, one must recognize that the picture emerging from Josephus and Philo is very different from that conveyed by the Dead Sea Scrolls. Josephus and Philo were versed in Greek philosophy, as is apparent throughout. The Dead Sea Scrolls, on the other hand, virtually exclude the possibility of reincarnation as an Essene belief.

The best and fullest account of the Essenes from Greco-Roman antiquity is found in Josephus, *The Jewish War* 2. 120–161. Here they are represented as similar to the Pythagorean communities in both belief and practice. The Greek text with facing pages of English translation is widely available in the Loeb Classical Library, published by Harvard University Press.

Philo's discussion of the Essenes is less extensive than that of Josephus and deals only with their style of life. He discusses them in *Every Good Man Is Free* 75–91 and the *Hypo-*

thetica 11.1–18. Both of these works are in the Loeb Classical Library Edition of Philo, Vol. IX.

For those interested in the contrast provided by the Dead Sea Scrolls, I would recommend *The Dead Sea Scriptures*, rev. ed., by Theodor H. Gaster (Doubleday Anchor Book, 1956).

THE EARLY CHURCH

The concept of the preexistence of the soul is suggested by Origen's predecessor, Clement of Alexandria. A Christian Platonist, he was not as speculative as Origen in his theology and did not attract the censure of later ecclesiasts. See Clement's *Exhortation to the Heathen* 1.6 for a very clear statement of preexistence. His works are available in *The Ante-Nicene Fathers*, Vol. II (Wm. B. Eerdmans, 1962).

The controversy that finally closed the door on preexistence grew around the works of Origen. In the anathemas against his work, *On First Principles*, one can see the final collision between orthodoxy and Origenism. For preexistence, see *On First Principles* 1.4.1. For the possibility of *karma*, see *On First Principles* 1.8.4 and 2.9.7. For an unmistakable statement of reincarnation, see *On First Principles* 1.8.4 and 2. 8.3. These references are to G. W. Butterworth's English translation, formerly available as a Harper Torchbook and now published by the Peter Smith Press.

The opponents of Origen were Methodius of Olympus, whose *On the Resurrection* is in *The Ante-Nicene Fathers*, Vol. VI; Epiphanius of Salamis, who deals with Origen in sections 100–109 of his *Ancoratus*, not available in English, but to be found in Greek with adjoining Latin translation in Migne *PG* 43; Theophilus of Alexandria, whose letters in Greek against Origen are preserved only in the Latin translation of Jerome, in *The Nicene and Post-Nicene Fathers*, Second Series, Vol. VI (Wm. B. Eerdmans) the Emperor Justinian, whose articles of condemnation from the year 543 are in sections 203–211 of Heinrich Denzinger's *The Sources of Catholic Dogma* (B. Herder Book Company, 1957).

CONTEMPORARY LITERATURE

There is a voluminous literature from the esoteric and psychic sponsors of reincarnation. Since, however, these have played no direct role in the composition of this book, I shall not mention them here.

For the serious reader on reincarnation, there are two recent studies that I would recommend highly. These are Ian Stevenson's *Twenty Cases Suggestive of Reincarnation* (American Society for Psychical Research, New York, 1966), discussed in Chapter II of the present work, and *Reincarnation in World Thought*, by Joseph Head and S. L. Cranston (Julian Press, 1969). The latter, a gargantuan work of research, offers an extensive survey of statements on reincarnation throughout the world and throughout the ages.